A Taste of Somerset

Dedicated to
Family, Friends
and a dog called Bertie

To Barbs
With love from
The Author xx 17 August 2008

A Taste of Somerset

FINE FOOD and RECIPES

ANDREA LEEMAN

photography by
Stephen Morris

 *redcliffe*

A Cream Legbar at Fenton Farm

First published in 2004 by Redcliffe Press Ltd, 81g Pembroke Road, Bristol BS8 3EA
Tel: 0117 973 7207 e.mail: johnsansom@aol.com
© Andrea Leeman (text) Stephen Morris (photographs)

ISBN 1 904537 00 6

British Library Cataloguing-in-Publication Data
A catalogue record for this book is available from the British Library.

Design and typesetting by Stephen Morris Communications: smc@freeuk.com Bristol and Liverpool, and printed by HSW Print, Tonypandy, Rhondda.

cover photograph: Robin Small, Charlton Orchards
title page: Bridgwater Bay

Ingredients

Liz Scott's Aberdeen Angus

Introduction

Food and drink have always been my game. Life as a restaurateur in Chelsea and at the Open Air Theatre in London's Regent's Park presented a deliciously colourful, if sometimes chaotic existence; ultimately it led to magazine work and a change of location to Bristol. The time felt right to think about a cookery book, but professional advice on the matter was succinct – don't think of it without a sound peg upon which to hang the project. An idea began to gel. Somerset was the perfect subject. Somerset is the county that offers not only superb cheeses, apples and cider, but produces an abundance of superlative foods from dairy produce and meats to smoked eels and asparagus.

During a truly extraordinary year I met and talked to many growers, farmers and producers whilst zigzagging the county through frosts, rain and the glorious summer of 2003 – and falling more in love by the moment with the variety of scenery. The descents from the Mendip Hills to the uniquely flat landscape of the Somerset Levels, the hidden villages and low, square church towers with their fine finials. The book came to life because of the dedication of everyone I met, all of whom have put their futures on the line to follow their instincts and offer privilege of access to top-quality ingredients. This is a county where the Farmers' Markets flourish, although there's a way to go before we use them with the aplomb of the French.

The recipes in *A Taste of Somerset* are an eclectic mix – dishes I cook at home that allow good ingredients to speak for themselves. They adhere to season and simplicity, following the current healthy interest shown by consumers to source the best of local produce, rather than relying totally on supermarkets.

Finally, a heartfelt apology to those not included in the book. Time and space called the tune, so a host of stories of enterprise and success remain, as yet, untold.

Huxy Ducks

Arne Herbs

Anthony Lyman-Dixon · Arne Herbs · Limeburn Nurseries · Limeburn Hill · Chew Magna · Bristol · BS40 8QW
Tel: 01275 333399 web: www.arneherbs.co.uk

Anthony Lyman-Dixon

The telephone conversation ran thus:

'Can I come and see you?'

'I'm very busy.'

'When would be a good time?'

'There's never a good time.'

'OK, when should I be the least nuisance?'

'You'll always be a nuisance......'

The visit took place the following afternoon, by appointment of course. Anthony Lyman-Dixon emerged from his nursery clad in several layers of woolly jumper, liberally holed but patched by yet a further layer beneath. Here was an enthusiast *par excellence*, professorial in his approach and perfectly delightful as a guide and tutor. I asked what had set him on the herb trail.

Mr Lyman-Dixon is an academic, he lectures on herbs, he is a fount of knowledge about medicinal herbs and an expert on historic medieval, renaissance, and Tudor herbs and plants, and he is also a world expert on lavender. He points out that almost every plant in a medieval garden was dual-purpose, both medicinal and edible. In the 1960s he was in Italy and learnt to cook in cheap restaurants where ingredients were simple and herbs came by the fistful. On returning to England he heard the twentieth-century doyenne of cookery, Elizabeth David, claim that you simply couldn't get fresh basil in England. Anthony took up the challenge and began a horticultural life with a pack of Robert Carrier Mixed Herb seeds. In a reflective moment he added that butterfly herbs were another speciality: 'you see in 1880 I had an uncle in Montreal who was keen on butterflies'. The Lyman Museum in Montreal was founded in 1914 as the result of Henry H Lyman's work on entomology and Canadian *lepidoptera*.

Rows of regimented pots are not to be found, instead the poly-tunnels are a glorious concatenation of medicinal and edible, of thrift and thyme, Vietnamese coriander and sorrel. 'No decent Turk would make a moussaka without sorrel, wonderful with fatty old sheep.' He has entitled one particular poly-tunnel France in Exile; here lavender from the Garrigue mingles with Corsican rosemary and myrtle and is where young pomegranates thrive. The pomegranates were the result of a purchase of one fruit from Reg-the-Veg, a celebrated Clifton fruit and vegetable emporium. The former are the results of visits to his ex-wife in France who, he explains, is beating the French at their own game, cheese-making.

If herbs are your interest, then Arne Herbs are unmissable. Don't expect advice on herbal cures as A L-D points out that it would be illegal for him to give this. Do telephone beforehand, particularly if you want specific plants. He and his assistant Jenny Thomas, an authority on potagers (kitchen gardens), run Arne Herbs dual-handed so a little warning of an intended visit is much appreciated.

Cherryfield Asparagus

Stephen Crossman · Cherryfield Asparagus · Court Place · Withycombe · Somerset · TA24 6QB
Tel: 01984 640236

Don't miss the English asparagus season, it's one of the great but short-lived luxury crops grown in the U.K. and traditionally runs from early in May until June 21st, the longest day. However if the crop shows signs of stress by sending up only the spindly little shoots known as sprue, the harvest stops earlier.

The red, iron-rich Somerset soil of Steve Crossman's fields is within sight of the Bristol Channel – and the red-ridged fields of soil are just about all you do see during the season. As soon as the luscious green spears emerge, a V-shaped cutting knife is used to sever them just below ground level. Steve fell in love with the flavour when a boy and describes the plants as athletes with the endurance of a long distance runner. During the initial growing season when the asparagus is being cut and if the weather's warm – warmth is crucial to its metabolism – spears can grow up to eight inches in twenty-four hours. When cutting stops towards the end of June, the plants send up their ferns and gather all the necessary nutrition for the next season within the ensuing three months.

The Dutch have done most of the breeding in modern times although originally asparagus was probably from Thailand or Burma; it's typically a seaside plant so consequently high levels of salt don't bother it too much and of course salt is also a good weed killer. Good plantations last 12-13 years, attacked sometimes by the little black-and-yellow

Stephen Crossman

backed asparagus beetle that eats into the plant to lay its eggs, but the beetle in turn becomes a good dinner for the ladybirds. Roots go 3-4 feet down and escape most frost, at the same time gathering nutrients and moisture.

There's a swing in Europe away from the white asparagus seen particularly in Germany and France. In fact it's exactly the same plant but shoots are cut well below ground level before they form chlorophyll by being exposed to daylight. In the days of chamber pots under the beds, asparagus was known as housemaids' horror because it causes the urine to smell so dreadful, although the ability to smell it seems to be genetically controlled so not everyone suffers.

When buying asparagus, look for good straight spears with a neat head to them, and if you want to store it for a few days, wrap in a damp cloth and keep in the fridge. Steve Crossman sells all his from the door. During the season they are open from 10.00am to 6.00pm, seven days a week, but it's always worth ringing to check in advance – and certainly if it's a big order. The farm's early-crop Irish Ulster Sceptre potatoes are available in June, highly recommended for their flavour and also available at the door. Take a trip into Minehead or Taunton and you can also buy the farm's pork from Gerald David the butcher (*see* page 106).

Brown and Forrest

Brown and Forrest · Bowdens Farm · Hambridge · Somerset · TA10 OBP
Tel: 01458 250875   e.mail: brownforrest@btinternet.com

In 1981 Michael Brown and his wife set up their smoke house just outside Langport. Previously Michael sold eels to the Dutch before they became the inspiration for his Somerset-based enterprise. The extraordinary odyssey of the Silver Migratory Eels begins in breeding grounds in the Sargasso Sea from whence the young eels or elvers drift on the Gulf Stream for three years or so before reaching European shores. From here they head up every available freshwater outlet.

The River Severn's wide entrance acts like a giant funnel and once into the river, the elvers take up residence in sub-sidiary rivers and streams for anything up to twenty years. On a delectable diet of earth worms, crustaceans, alder fly and fish eggs, they grow to maturity, fending off predators ranging from coarse fish and trout to birds, herons and otters, and, yes of course, the human variety. The Spanish, for example, use tonnes of *anguilas* each year and the Japanese are mad about them. A friend from Gloucester remembers as a child going with her family, carrying an enamel bowl to the quay to be filled with elvers. The cost, a shilling a bowl. Today three figures would be nearer the mark and Gloucester folk no longer feast on their local delicacy as the catch is exported. Elvers must be eaten when very small before the skins darken. A favourite old way of cooking them was to sizzle in bacon fat, serve with a splash of vinegar and mop up the juices with a hunk of bread.

As plump adults, akin to many migratory birds, eels close down their digestive systems to prepare for returning to the Sargasso. They are shy of light and the running of the eel takes place at night when the moon is low, and towards the latter end of the year some will even travel overland to begin this journey. The river keepers are alert for the exodus and the eels are largely caught near the mills where the water can be controlled. Racks with metal frames like toothcombs are used for the trapping.

After the catch, the eels are blast-frozen; this treatment allows safe storage until they are required for smoking and the freezing makes it much easier to remove the tough and slimy protective coating. Once gutted, the eels are brined for 2-3 hours in salt solution, then hot-smoked for 15 minutes followed by 1 hour of cold smoking over beech and apple wood.

For me, smoked eel surpasses almost all other delicacies. Brown and Forrest have a delightfully informal restaurant attached to the smokery where, for a modest sum, you can sit down to a plate of eel on rye bread with salad, served as Michael Brown recommends – with a squeeze of fresh lemon, black pepper and maybe a little horseradish and beetroot pickle. Local apple juice is a good accompaniment; alterna-tively a crisp Sauvignon Blanc wine. There are not many recipes suitable for smoked eels without spoiling its texture and flavour, but the Danes like to serve it with *Aeg Stand*, strips of savoury egg custard made very thinly like an

omelette (see page 58) – and of course they would wash it down with a glass of iced Aquavit.

Brown and Forrest sell other excellent smoked products such as salmon, local venison, duck and chicken. The latest to join the menu is pork tenderloin, oak-smoked after marinating in local cider – and the now famous Somerset Cider Brandy.

Michael Brown

Cedar Walk Farms

Leighton Lane Industrial Estate · Evercreech · Shepton Mallet · BA4 6LQ · Tel: 01749 830800 Fax: 01749 831000
e.mail: sales@cedarwalk.com web: www.cedarwalk.com

Cedar Walk specialises in traditional breeds of poultry, pork, lamb and beef and wild game.

Neil Macdonald began life as a cereal farmer, but took a sharp career turn after he and his wife reared three piglets in their dog kennel. He realised many of the traditional breeds of animals offered higher quality and more flavoursome meats because their development is slower, and don't lend themselves to speedy commercial production. These animals can be reared only on an extensive free-range system.

The Cedar Farm enterprise is in its infancy. Grazing covers 250 acres of which 200 acres are run as ranch land with animals brought into the farm only once or twice a year (apart from pigs, lowland breeds of sheep, and poultry). The mission of the farm is to produce star quality meat, so the way the animals are reared, slaughtered, hung and butchered are stages of equal importance. To enhance flavour and eliminate infection in oven poultry after slaughter, birds are plucked and hung 'dry'

for three days; wet plucking spreads infection and lessens shelf life. Including curing and sausage making, all their butchering is done on the premises. Sales of Cedar Walk Farms' meats are reliant on the Farmers' and Council Markets and on mail order, so what the customer really wants rules when it comes to types of cuts – lamb and pork leg-steaks top the bill of favourites. Taken from prime joints of meat, these are simple and quick to cook at the end of a long day.

Until my visit to Cedar Walk, the significance of the size of a pig's ear had seemed immaterial. Neil Macdonald scratched the head of his Gloucester Old Spot and discussed the merits and otherwise of the rare pig breeds such as Saddlebacks and Middle Whites. It seems the disappearing act performed by another rare breed, the famous Tamworth

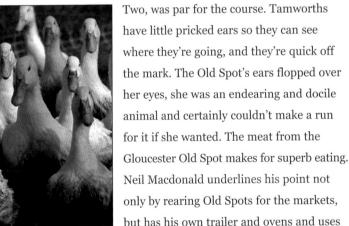

Two, was par for the course. Tamworths have little pricked ears so they can see where they're going, and they're quick off the mark. The Old Spot's ears flopped over her eyes, she was an endearing and docile animal and certainly couldn't make a run for it if she wanted. The meat from the Gloucester Old Spot makes for superb eating. Neil Macdonald underlines his point not only by rearing Old Spots for the markets, but has his own trailer and ovens and uses them for hog roasts at various functions.

The motto of the farm is 'Look after the soil. The soil will look after the animals. The animals will look after you.' So why haven't Cedar Farms gone the whole hog and become organic? They pay a lot of attention to the quality of the grassland and its trace elements and use a three-year rotation with their free-range poultry, greatly reducing risks from salmonella. The reason is simple: the paper-work and rubber-stamping involved in organic farming is a nightmare. So Neil chose a middle way, feeding and caring for the animals and poultry to a tremendously high standard, avoiding food additives but using antibiotics if an animal becomes seriously sick. The main aim of Cedar Walk Farms is the eating quality, texture and flavour, not always apparent in organic production.

We went to a field to see a huddle of the farm's Huxy ducklings on their first day out. This unusual breed provides a substantial ratio of meat to carcass and not too much fat, so it's popular with consumers. Incidentally, the collective noun for duck standing around is a Raft of Duck – and if they're in a pond, a Paddling of Duck.

Gloucester Old Spot

Bath Soft Cheese

Graham and Gabrielle Padfield · Park Farm · Kelston · Bath · BA1 9AG
Tel: 01225 331601

There is a timeless charm about the countryside around Kelston, midway between Bath and Bristol and tucked inside the county boundary with Gloucestershire. Graham Padfield is the third generation of his family to farm in this village and like other dairy farmers of late, he's suffered the constriction of milk quotas. He says they've fossilised dairy farming. Since January 2003 he is registered as an organic farmer with a herd of 160 Friesian cattle and has now diversified so that most of his milk yield goes into cheese making. At present excess milk is sold to an organic-oriented milk co-operative, but in time he wants to use all of it for cheese.

Park Farm makes four types of cheese, Bath Soft Cheese, Bath Triple Cream, Bath Blue Cheese and also a goat cheese. The two soft cheeses mature within 4-7 weeks, shifted from the dairy on reed mats to the cool store before final transference to stainless steel wires, all the while developing the characteristic white mould associated with soft cheeses.

The buttercup-coloured Bath Triple Cream laced with Jersey cream is rich and buttery, quite different from the Bath Soft cheese which is more savoury and flowing in character when fully ripe, perfect with crusty bread and a glass of local beer. The shelf-life of white mould cheese is much shorter than a hard cheese, perhaps under ideal conditions four weeks: hard cheeses generally last longer as they shuffle off potentially harmful pathogens as the cheese matures.

The making of Bath Blue, a subtle Stilton-like cheese, involves the addition of blue mould spores to the milk at the beginning of the cheese-making process. These moulds can only develop in the presence of air, hence blue cheeses are spiked to facilitate access to oxygen. The blue spiking line is often obvious when cutting a wedge from a blue cheese.

Not only are Park Farm's cheeses fine quality and very individual, a great deal of thought has gone into packaging and marketing, most notably the Bath Soft Cheese in its waxy paper and parchment sleeve with distinguished black graphics and red seal. The farm is a family business and packaging is in the hands of Gabrielle Padfield, while artwork is looked after by one of their four children, Felix, who studied at St Martin's School of Art.

There is no direct sales outlet at the farm, but the cheeses are available from the Bath Farmers' Market, several delicatessens including the Bath Fine Cheese Company, Paxton & Whitfield and the Chandos Delies in Bath and Bristol, along with Waitrose supermarkets throughout Somerset. Park Farm does offer a mail order service: a great idea for presents (tel. 01225 331601). It's also a delightful bed and breakfast in beautiful countryside and near to Bath. There are two available rooms: tel: 01225 424139.

Burcott Mill

Lesley and Ian Burt · Burcott Mill · Wookey · Near Wells · Somerset · BA5 1NJ
Tel: 01749 6733118   Fax: 01749 677376   e.mail: theburts@burcottmill.com

The twenty-first-century Miller of Burcott took up his post in the year 2000 following what he describes as a quest to get away from the corporate wilderness in London and back to reality. He is an enthusiast and well versed in the history of his mill, so the best way to introduce him is to borrow this short extract from his guidebook.

Today we are both a commercial mill and a working museum, spanning 1,900 years of history. A tribute to Roman design and Victorian engineering. We use a 1,000-year-old water channel to operate 140-year-old machinery, to produce handcrafted flour which is the key ingredient in award-winning breads.

The family livestock of guinea pigs, ducklings, hens and a strutting chanticleer inhabit the mill's entrance, all beneficiaries of the overspills of grain. The visit was a revelation for everyone, whether to admire the mechanics, the great water wheel and the Roman leat or millstream – or just to savour the homely smell of newly milled flour. While the Victorian machinery manoeuvres gracefully through its paces, the grain, fed by a hopper, trickles into a wooden feed shoe – a metal spindle vibrates the shoe to control the speed flow to the millstones. The jiggling noise of the shoe reminded the Victorians of chattering, so they called the spindle 'a damsel' and the feed shoe 'a chatterbox', hence the origin of the word.

The grain milled at Burcott comes from East Anglia where it tends to have a higher-than-national average protein content and makes excellent wholemeal flour, suitable for bread making. Most of Ian Burt's flour finds its way to homes exactly as it would have done a hundred years ago and is also used by several local bakers. I beg you not to leave without purchasing a bag.

The ingenuity of the mill's mechanics is pin-pointed when the machinery is closed down at the end of the day: a procedure unchanged since Roman times and one that, astonishingly, takes seconds rather than minutes and is done with fingertip control. First the grain flow is stopped, the giant millstones are separated by a turn of a handle, the gate feeding water to the wheel is closed and the sluice gate opened to empty the millstream and allow the water to tumble away down into the river Axe below. Silence.

The mill is open from Easter until the end of September (except on Mondays, including Bank Holiday Mondays) and is on the B3139 near Wookey, not to be confused with Wookey Hole. In October it opens at weekends. The Burts also have six rooms and offer discounts if you stay more than one night. After breakfast you are welcome to join the miller for a private tour of Burcott Mill.

Ian Burt

Cotleigh Brewery

Ford Road · Wiveliscombe · Somerset · TA4 2RE Tel: 01984 624086 Fax: 01984 624365
e.mail: cotleigh@cloveruk.net

Thanks to prolonged success, Cotleigh Brewery is now well ensconced in its third home since its beginning in 1979. Founders John and Jennifer Aries handed over the reins to Steve Heptinstall and Fred Domellof in 2003, both newcomers to brewing. Although well-versed in the food and drink business, both are pleased the Aries will remain to hand on a consultancy basis until at least 2005.

Cotleigh's flagship beer is Tawny, the first brand name used by Mr and Mrs Aries and still accounting for fifty per cent of the company's business. Most of the beers follow a bird theme as the brewery has a long association with the Hawk and Owl Trust and feel they can help raise awareness and finance for the association. Golden Eagle, Barn Owl and Tawny are available for twelve months of the year and the darker Old Buzzard comes into play during the six winter months. Reinbeer is one seasonal exception to the bird rule.

Hops mostly come from Herefordshire, from RG and MD Thomas in Leominster; not only does the brewery buy from the same farmer every year, the hops come from the same corner of the same field in order to maintain a consistency of flavour. Once the hops are dried, they are vacuum-packed to preserve flavours. Barley is from Tuckers Maltings in Devon. Having the opportunity to chew on a few grains of their malted barley brought back memories of those malty bedtime drinks.

Cotleigh's procedure for making beer is thus: the malted barley is ground to grist and put into a large container called a mash tun where it steeps in hot water to extract from the grist the malt and sugar that will later become alcohol. The spent grain is used for cattle feed and the sugary liquid, now called wort, is run off into a copper like a huge kettle. In here the hops are added. The first charge of hops gives the beer its bitterness and the second impacts the nose. The liquid boils for an hour and stands for a further twenty minutes to let the unwanted proteins and hops settle. Next comes the fermentation. The wort runs into a tank where yeast is added and the beer now takes up the status of a brew, fermenting for about four days. Removing the yeast from the top and cooling the liquid to 14°C stop the fermentation. The racking or moving the beer into casks is the final stage, after which it stays in store for about two weeks for cask conditioning when a secondary fermentation occurs.

Outlets for Cotleigh beers are throughout freehouses in Somerset, Devon, Dorset and Cornwall, roughly within a fifty-mile radius of the brewery. It is also possible to buy from the Brewery door but orders need to be placed twenty fours in advance; the smallest unit available is a polypin (36 pints). Within the very near future Cotleigh plan to supply bottled beer and a range of branded wines. If visiting Wiveliscombe and overcome by thirst for a pint of this excellent beer, head for the Bear in the centre of town where there are four Cotleigh beers on tap.

Charlton Orchards

Robin and June Small, Duncan Small and Sally Bail · Charlton Orchards · Creech St. Michael · Taunton · TA3 5PF
Tel: 01823 412959/412979

September 30th was an Indian summer day and according to folk law the last chance in the year to pick blackberries before the witches do unmentionable things to them. With the apple harvest in full swing, I stood in the unloading yard with Robin and June Small watching the wooden boxes of fruit coming in from the orchards and batting away the odd wasp. Charlton also grow pears, plums, damsons, red, white and blackcurrants, raspberries and strawberries. More recently herbs have been added to the production list, including twelve varieties of mint.

The laden fruit trees are from the pages of a children's book. Expert grafting has increased yields and intermittent plantings of crab apples act as pollinators, helped by wild and hive bees. The local beekeeper sends his hives to the orchards for spring and summer, hence the good honey sold in Charlton's shop. For small-garden enthusiasts, some of the trees have been espaliered – pruned to grow along trellised wires – while others have been cordoned – grown as single stems in order to show what bumper crops can be harvested from minimal spaces. Fruit trees have obvious adversaries like birds and deer but for the apple, codling moths are the worst enemy; the moths lay eggs in the blossom and feed on the young fruits. To keep spraying to a minimum and to

determine the extent of the problem, small sticky trays implanted with a pheromone irresistible to the male moth hang here and there in the trees. If the head count on the sticky pads is excessive, only then is it deemed necessary to treat the trees.

The heart of the orchard contains some of the oldest varieties of apples, the most ancient of which is Court Pendu Plat with a lineage from 1613. The apple is rich, sweet-scented and at its peak in December and January. Robin Small's favourite is a handsome Orlean's Reinette, russet-skinned and with a dense fruit flavour he likens to walnuts. His advice is 'eat it for pleasure – forget television, bring out the Stilton cheese and open a bottle of port'. He said nothing much goes to waste in the orchard. In winter deer, redwings, pheasants, rabbits, badgers and others feed from the fruits that have to be dumped at the end of the season.

Apples peak at various times in the autumn and New Year. Late pickers need time to mature so Charlton has a big cold store where the fruit stays in ideal conditions. In addition to the shop selling apple juice, their own pickles, honey and of course all their other varieties of fruits according to season, they have events which include an Apple Day and a Tasting

Robin Small

June Small

Louis, one of a group of young people from Fairbridge*

Day. The latter is in December and it's the opportunity for everyone to try the new jams, pickles and fruits. Charlton's advice for Christmas is to forego gooey chocolates and send friends a box of juicy mixed apples instead.

*__Fairbridge__ is a UK-based charitable organisation that gives socially-excluded young people a new lease on life.

Butcombe Brewery

Butcombe · Bristol · BS40 7QX
Tel: 01275 472240

Beer and public houses alike have seen change since the days of the frosted glass that shielded the men from the over-watchful eye of their womenfolk. There was a period when the big brewers looked like scuppering the existence of small local breweries, and lager would lure away the real ale drinkers. CAMRA, the Campaign for Real Ale, worked hard to regenerate interest in good ale, their efforts rewarded by small breweries such as Butcombe, making ale with character and style. A fundamental difference between lager and ale is the use of different yeasts; lager is bottom-fermented whereas ale is top-fermented, meaning the yeast rises to the top of the liquid after the fermentation. Another difference is that lager is stored for a long time in maturation vessels, *lager* being German for store. Only Britain and Ireland produce cask-conditioned ale in any quantity, yet the casks are no longer made here and have to be imported.

A man who learned his brewing techniques courtesy of Guinness and Courage, Simon Whitmore started Butcombe Brewery in derelict farm buildings in 1978. The local planning officer looked askance at an application for industry in the green belt, but proved himself a valuable ally when he suggested the planning committee would be amenable to the phrase *rural craft*. The brewery changed hands in 2003 and is now owned by Guy Newell and Paul Horsley with a number of friendly shareholders; Guy and Paul are newcomers to the brewing business but are taking their technical guidelines from Simon Whitmore who will remain part-time for the next year or so. During this period the brewery will move premises to a more suitable site nearby.

The dictionary definition of beer is 'an alcoholic drink made from yeast-fermented malt flavoured with hops'. Ergo, the important ingredients for good beer are malted barley, hops and water. Brewers look for barley with low protein; high-protein grain makes the beer cloudy. Butcombe buys a variety called Marris Otter, delivered ready-malted from north Norfolk. The hops are grown in Kent: good hops are scarce and growers need encouragement, so Butcombe's orders go as far ahead as 2007. It's the hops that cause the bittering effect in beer and flavours change from variety to variety. The water is straight from the tap; in other words, Mendip water requiring little treatment other than an addition of calcium sulphate, alias gypsum. The latter is a characteristic found in water from the River Trent and nearby boreholes – Burton-on-Trent was once the home of all the great beer names and adding gypsum to the water is known as Burtonising. The gypsum gives beer a dry flavour.

Butcombe brews two sorts of beer – Butcombe Bitter, a dry, clean hoppy beer at 4.0 abv and Butcombe Gold, a traditional warm and mellow beer, 4.7 abv*. Distribution takes place within a fifty-miles radius by the brewery's own lorries, although not north of the M4. Further afield, wholesale and pub-owning companies take over delivery. Whereas tastes for lager are national or even international, demands for different brands of real ale tend to be local or regional. If you fancy supping a pint of this nectar in a Butcombe-owned pub, there is a choice of six throughout the county. The Ring O' Bells at Compton Martin, The Swan at Rowberrow, The Lamb at Axbridge, The Bell at Hillgrove Street (off Stokes Croft in Bristol), The Old Crown at Kelston and the Red Tile at Cossington, north of Bridgwater.

Please ring beforehand to buy wholesale direct from the brewery. Quantities come in polypins (4 ½ gallons) or in firkins (9 gallons). The brewery is open on weekdays and on Saturdays until 12.00 noon.

* Abv: alcohol by volume. This is the French *Gay Lussac* system of expressing the alcoholic content of drinks in proportional terms.

Andrew Gabriel

Andrew Gabriel · Fenton Farm · Holcombe Rogus · near Wellington · Somerset · TA21 0NF
Tel: 01823 672075 e.mail: fentonpoultry@aol.com web: www.fentonpoultry.co.uk

If I'm reincarnated as a chicken, then save me a perch at Fenton Farm. On a clear day the view is to infinity, taking in the Blackdown Hills, the Mendips and the Quantocks and beyond, deep into Devon. Fenton Farm is in fact marginally inside the Devon border, despite its Somerset post-code.

In 2003 Andrew Gabriel received a Small Producers Award from Waitrose and *The Times*, in the category of Best Newcomer and winner of the Fresh Produce section. Born on the adjacent family farm, he initially pursued the tradition of arable, beef and turkey farming. Then his wife suggested keeping hens, a logical move as much of the necessary equipment was already in place thanks to the presence of the turkeys.

Part of the farm was once stables and now provides ideal, airy conditions for rearing young poultry. Two or so years ago saw the arrival of the first batch of twenty Araucana chickens,

a rare-breed whose roots are in Chile. Beautiful birds sporting a palette of plumage from black and metallic green to lavender, some crowned with punky topknots. To cap it all, they lay blue-green eggs with rich yellow yolks. Andrew Gabriel is now breeding his own Araucanas, bringing in new cockerels every now and again to keep the stock strong.

His Hybrid Marans, alias Speckledys, are responsible for

Andrew Gabriel

White Leghorn

dark brown eggs whilst the White Leghorns produce shells as white as bone china. In the orchard, hens scratch around beneath the apple trees. Three smart-looking cockerels stride up and down a run. Andrew pointed to a particular bird with a crimson comb and a galvanising yellow eye, 'my killer cockerel, he'll even have a go at me'. Feed is GM-free and natural, while the wheat the birds eat is also grown on the farm.

In terms of business risk, from the breeding angle only two-thirds of eggs hatch out and it's twenty weeks before the first pullet eggs are laid. The resident team of Collie dogs work as an effective deterrent to the foxes, showing masterful restraint – and just an occasional lick of the lips when amongst the poultry.

Fenton Farm also supplies poultry from day-old chicks through to point-of-lay as well as White, Bronze and Norfolk Black turkeys for Christmas. Two brown, two white and two blue eggs are beautifully packaged in bright pink egg boxes which are available from The Cheese and Wine Shop in Wellington, The County Stores in Taunton and Williton, Wallaces the farm shop in Hemyock, and Riverside Butchers in Taunton. If you are interested in visiting or would like advice, please telephone the farm.

Exmoor Blue Cheese

Ian and Ruby Arnett · Exmoor Blue Cheese Ltd · Willett Farm · Lydeard St Lawrence · Taunton · TA4 3QB
Tel: 01984 667328   Fax: 01984 667314   e.mail: bluecheese@btclick.com

On the slopes of the Brendon Hills on the edge of Exmoor, Ian and Ruby Arnett lease one of the buildings at Willett Farm to make their Exmoor Blue cheese. Or, to be more accurate, 'cheeses' as the milk comes from Jersey and Friesian cows, goats, sheep – and buffalo. Yes, there are buffalo in the West Country! All the milks are turned into blue cheeses, medium soft in style – and all are unpasteurised.

This was a bleak winter day with rain lashing the yard outside the dairy, and combined with the chill inside the dairy it brought home the dedication required in producing such handmade cheeses – but this is the way Ian Arnett and his wife see the future. They want to retain the personal 'hands-on' stage as the business develops.

In keeping with other styles of blue cheese, the blue mould goes into the milk at the same time as the rennet at the beginning of the process, because with modern cheese-making methods the desirable blue moulds don't happen naturally. Their subsequent maturation time varies from four to ten weeks.

When asked advice on keeping cheeses in an ideal condition, Ian suggests this would be in an old-fashioned larder on a marble slab, and, if possible, using greaseproof paper rather than cling film. He also points out that milk for his Exmoor Blue Cheese must come from cows grazing inside the Exmoor National Park which falls under the heading of PGI, Protected Geographical Indication. The Jersey Exmoor Blue is very creamy and piquant all at the same time.

Although there is no farm shop, cheeses are available locally from the Bridgwater and Minehead Farmers' Markets, Sara's Dairy (Taunton, Illminster and Bridgwater) and The Larder in Wellington.

Lighthouse Ice Cream

Emma Pusill · Lighthouse Ice Cream · 272 Berrow Road · Berrow · Somerset · TA8 2JH
Tel: 01278 782634   Mob: 07717 293947   e.mail: lighthouseicecream@hotmail.com

Emma Pusill's Lighthouse Ice Cream business is a recently launched enterprise; when we met in the picturesque Axbridge market, it had been in operation for only a few months. Emma makes the ice cream in her own kitchen, using natural ingredients, locally sourced if possible. Cream comes from Rookery Farm Creamery (also available at Axbridge market), fruit from Cheddar Vale Nurseries, Stawell Fruit Farm and Charlton Orchards, and free range eggs from Westcroft Farm Eggs in Berrow. Even the printing, labelling and tubs come through local suppliers.

Although in its infancy, the purity of this delicious ice cream must ensure it a flourishing future. Emma has an à la carte list, as well as flavours that make a seasonal appearance. Even in shivering pre-Christmas weather when stallholders were trying to blow life into numb fingers, the Christmas Pudding ice cream was a sell-out; I was fortunate enough to purchase the last of the Late Season Damson.

There is a free delivery service within a ten-mile radius of Burnham on Sea, and future plans include selling to independent retailers. Should you lust after a particular flavour, Emma will make it to order; likewise she offers to make ice cream from home-grown fruit.

James's Chocolates

Lower Westcombe Farm · Evercreech · Shepton Mallet · Somerset · BA4 6ER
Tel: 01749 831330 Fax: 01749 831370

A year or so ago I came upon the newly opened Bar Chocolat in Bristol. The day was bitingly cold, designed for drinking good hot chocolate; such was the transcendental experience that it came as something of a surprise to look from the café window and see Bristol's streets rather than snow-clad Swiss Alps. Subsequently, the Bar Chocolat has been joined by one in Bath and another within Selfridges in Birmingham. All sell selections of James's Chocolates.

Their creator James Hutchins trained as a biologist but found himself amongst his university friends in the role of birthday-cake maker. Chocolate cake was the big draw. He is a self-taught chocolatier and recounts early days when his first truffle recipes were cut-outs from magazines but over the years he's honed his own very individual style. Six years ago he moved to the Lower Westcombe Farm complex and is now settled in a converted stable.

Valentine's Day was looming large at the stable. Rock-like

blocks of French Valrhona and Belgium Callebaut chocolate lay in wait for melting, tempering and to be turned into objects of temptation, good enough to win hearts. James buys six to seven grades of chocolate that in turn deliver a thorough-going mix of cocoa solids; it's the blending and tempering (cooling and re-heating) of these that give his chocolate its particular style and gleaming finish.

Quality is not the only thing that makes these chocolates different. There is wit and originality about his work; amongst the fresh cream truffles, chocolate gingers and pralines lurk exotic green and red tropical fish, Gloucester Old Spot and Saddleback pigs, boxes of sardines dashed with bright blue – and chocolate mice good enough to make the girls scream. My favourite are the cylindrical packs of chocolate discs, orange and cardamom and hazelnut and cinnamon or fruit and nut decorated with pecan and almonds.

The nine-strong work force do everything by hand, right

down to the last twirl of ribbon on the packaging before distribution to outlets that include Bar Chocolat in Bristol and Bath, Fortnum and Mason, Heals, Selfridges, John Lewis and Waitrose. In Somerset stockists include The Delicatessen, 36 The High Street, Shepton Mallet BA4 5HS (tel: 01749 344523) and Emma B's, 6 West Street, Somerton TA11 7PS (tel: 01458 273444). The chocolates are not sold on site in the Westcombe Farm shop.

Special orders are available.

Jamie Montgomery

JA & E Montgomery Cheese Ltd · Manor Farm · North Cadbury · Yeovil · Somerset · BA22 7DW
Tel: 01963 440243

Cows grazing the land around Manor Farm feed from Arthurian soil. Cadbury Hill comes into the Doomsday Book as *Cadeberie* meaning a fortified hill – it's also thought to be the site of King Arthur's Camelot. When John Langman bought Manor Farm in 1910, cheese making had already been established and today the 1,300 acres are run by grandsons Jamie and his brother Archie Montgomery.

Think Montgomery's cheese, think fine artisan Cheddar; it was the moment to find out from the horse's mouth if Cheddar originated in Somerset and whether countries as far afield as Canada and New Zealand are entitled to call their cheese Cheddar. Jamie Montgomery gave a loyal-to-the-county answer: the land and climate in Somerset are ideal for cheese making because it's a wet county with good pastureland and minerals in the soil and it's also one of the milkiest counties. No one really knows where Cheddar originated but the 'cheddaring' is part of the cheese-making process, hence its name.

We headed for the dairy in time to find the morning's milk curded, cheddared and shredded. To begin making this unpasteurised cheese requires starter bacteria to which Jamie attaches great importance; a different starter is used every day of the week thus each day's cheese has an individual character. Montgomery's starters arrive frozen at -40°C and

thaw for a couple of days before required. Some cheese makers add them directly to the milk but at Manor Farm a churn of milk is sterilized the day before it's needed, injected with the starter and kept overnight, then added to the morning's milk. As soon as the first level of acidity is achieved in the milk – that which might be found in a calf's stomach – the rennet is added and about 50 minutes later the subsequent junket is ready to be cut with knives and stacked, the latter being the actual cheddaring process.

The cheese is shredded and moved to a gang press: this is similar to a row of large saucepans lying on their sides and pressurized at either end from whence the whey can drain. The following day the cheeses are dipped in very hot water to denature the protein on the outside of the cheese and help create a rind. Slightly molten lard helps to stick muslin to the cheese; it undergoes a further night in a press to secure the cloth before moving to the cheese store for 11 months' maturation.

The cheese store has a surreal beauty: dimly lit silhouettes of four thousand or more cheddars stand silent on the shelves while starbursts of moulds work around their girths devouring the lardy coating during their first three months in store. There's the pervading smell, a reminder of well-bred mousetrap, and of course ultimately the tasting. A cheese corer

Jamie Montgomery

makes it easy to probe out slim cylinders of cheeses and check their development, their creaminess, their saltiness and whether the perfect marriage of flavours had been achieved. This is superb Cheddar.

As well as a big potato crop 'sold to chippers on the south coast', Manor Farm has a small herd of Jersey cows and is running trials at present with a new cheese that's proving to be delectably rich and creamy. Watch this space for Ogle Shield. The farm is part of the first English Slow Food Presidium in association with Neal's Yard Dairy, London. Jamie reckons Slow Food won't change his market but it will fix it by encouraging people to maintain good taste.

The farm is not open to the public and rather than running a farm shop themselves, Manor Farm sell their cheeses through the local Post Office. In existence since 1850 and named Bristol House, the Post Office was a stopping point for the old Bristol/Southampton coach – 6 Woolston Road, North Cadbury, Somerset BA22 7DW (tel: 01963 440201). Other outlets include independent grocers, Neal's Yard, London, Harrods, Fortnums and Selfridges.

Brendan Sellick

Brendan Sellick · Mud Horse Cottage · Stolford · Near Cannington · Somerset · TA5 1TW
Tel: 01278 652297

Put your shirt on it, the Mud Horse won't make it to the finishing post at Wincanton. In Somerset speak, it's akin to a wooden sledge used by Brendan Sellick, fisherman on the Bristol Channel and someone whose work depends on crossing the mud flats at low tide to retrieve his catch. The mud horse is the nag that carries him to the haul waiting for him in the nets.

Brendan Sellick is the fourth generation in his family to use a mud horse and, reassuringly, his son Adrian is following in his footsteps. Despite his youthful air and obvious fitness, Mr Sellick is reaching three score years and ten. 'Once upon a time there were seven or eight families fishing this way but the numbers have dwindled, even twenty five years ago there were three families. You see, what you have to do is to lean into the horse and paddle it along with your feet, you need tight-grip shoes – it's a bitterly cold job in winter.' His great-grandfather had been a steeplejack and had taken up the business originally.

On a grisly day, this part of the Bristol Channel is very grey; Hinkley Point Power Station looms just along the shore. The call of the curlew adds a mournful air but another local inhabitant of Stolford talked enthusiastically of the bird life, including a sighting of whimbrels, breaking their journey *en route* for North Africa. Brendan Sellick reminisces about the summers in the old days before the council shipped in the enormous stone defences, when the natural stones on the beach bleached out white in the sun and the nets were laid on top to dry.

His nets are suspended from wooden posts out in the channel and are still mended and cared for in the same way today as they were four generations ago; fish are trapped on the ebbing tide. The mud horse is homemade, mostly of elm with a little deal. Bristol Channel has one of the biggest tidal variations in the world and the horse can only be operated at low water so the Sellicks don't fish on the neap tides when the water doesn't recede sufficiently; springs are best. His catch is the original fisherman's feast. Skate, cod, plaice, Dover soles, grey mullet – and brown shrimps, succulent little jobs that he pops into the cooking pot in his hut in the village and then peels by hand. If you don't want to eat them immediately, then pot them with melted butter, lemon juice, a little pepper and salt and serve with brown toast (*see* page 72).

There was an irresistible question, what had been the strangest catch ever? 'Well, when I was a lad, my father went out two or three days in a row, came back and said something was holing the nets. Next time they got 'im, a six-foot-long sturgeon. My father said to me, sit on him lad and we'll take your photograph, but I wouldn't do it, too scared see, this

Adrian Sellick

fish's gills were still going in and out, in and out, he were still alive. But we got the photo of him to this day, without me on it. I was only three at the time.'

Needless to say, catching Brendan Sellick is nearly as hard as catching a sturgeon. Do ring beforehand if you want to buy fish, and take a map with you. Stolford lies between Hinkley Point and Steart. Stogursey is the nearest sizeable village.

Monaghan Mushrooms

Monaghan Mushrooms · Stock Lane · Langford · Somerset · BS40 5ES
Tel: 01934 852751 sales office: 01934 852754 web: www.monaghan-mushrooms.com

This is a story far removed from Farmers' Markets. It describes the growing of *agaricus bisporus* and a harvest of three hundred thousand pounds in weight per week, 364 days a year, of which 90% of the crop goes to supermarkets. In other words, white and brown cup, button, open cup and flat mushrooms. Open cup and flat mushrooms are the button variety by another name, more growing time equals additional growth and a chance for the fruit to open.

Dieticians are in thrall to the mushroom: rich in water-soluble B group vitamins and minerals, mushrooms contain no sugar or starch, are cholesterol-free and have hardly a trace of fat, unless you fry them, of course. Ingredients for growth incorporate wheat straw, chicken manure and gypsum to which sphagnum peat and lime (previously used in the extraction of sugar from sugar beet) are later added as an over-layer, and all of which are ultimately returned to the land. To all intents and purposes most of this is pretty eco-friendly.

Graham Griffiths built the first mushroom farm on the site of the old Wrington Vale Nursery in the 1940s, a premises finally acquired by the Irish-based Monaghan Mushrooms in 1994. Monaghan are the biggest producers in the U.K. We begin our tour in the large yard where the compost so crucial for the colonisation of *mycelia*, the network of fine filaments or *hyphae* that constitute the rooting system for mushrooms, is prepared over a three-and-a-half week period. Donned in hard hat, overall and boots, mask to hand, we first see a goliath amongst machines churning layers of straw, chicken manure and gypsum, the latter preventing the compost from becoming too greasy. Proportions are 250 tonnes of straw to 150 of chicken manure. The smell is overpowering. Constant turning and fine tuning together with a smidgen of the old muck-and-magic achieves a temperature suitable for useful bacteria to begin to develop; what everyone wants is a nice homogenous mix prior to the pasteurisation to kill off pathogens and remove the ammonia.

The mushroom spores are impregnated onto sterilised grain, the grain then acts as a carrier and is introduced when the compost is cooled to 25°C. A conveyor-belt beds the mix on tiers of shelving like so many bunk beds set in warm arcades appropriately heated and cooled, monitored by state-of-the-art equipment and every aspect computer-recorded. The first indication of a flush, mushroom speak for a crop, is the appearance of miniscule white pin heads – the grand plan is to achieve two flushes per planting. The procedure from the first turning of the compost to the first flush is about two

Preparing the compost

months. Once the second flush is harvested, the arcade is sterilised and the compost sold as infill or for garden use.

Spooky? Yes, a little. The arcades are a humid Dali-esque world of white-capped heads wherever the eye falls in this twilight zone, although it's a myth that mushrooms need total darkness for growth. Two hundred and fifty pickers work in shifts to ensure optimum quality and packaging is done on the spot. Although there are no sales on the door, Monaghan are growing a hugely successful specialist product that finds its way through all sorts of outlets into just about every household and restaurant.

Mumfords Vineyard

Tony and Margaret Cox · Mumfords Vineyard · Shockerwick Lane · Bannerdown · Bath · BA1 7LQ
Tel: 01225 858367 Fax: 01225 852385

Mumfords' four acres of vineyard have a splendid view over the Avon Valley. The Bybrook, a tiny tributary of the Avon, runs along the bottom and houses fresh-water crayfish, at present both native and American although the latter are rapidly taking over in the rivers. It's late autumn and apart from a few pheasants zigzagging between the rows of vines, things are quiet. This year the pheasants have developed a palate for grapes and have vied in nuisance value with deer and badgers. A line of cricket-bat willow acts as a windbreak to ease the force of the sou'westerlies that can blow through the valley and wreak havoc with the vines, particularly at flowering time.

The vineyard is planted with vines designed to withstand the challenges of unpredictable English summers: Madeleine Angevine, Kerner, Reichensteiner and Triomphe. The latter is the vineyard's only red grape and is also used to help make Mumfords Rosé wine. Whereas 2002 was an averagely good vintage, the hot summer of 2003 resulted in fruit of unprecedented high quality but not a big yield. In good times when the flowering and fruit-set run to order, Madeleine Angevine is Mumfords' right-hand grape and produces up to 11,000 bottles. On a couple of occasions vines have even developed 'noble rot', a rich concentration of grape juice that occurs in late autumn and the style of which makes some of the great dessert wines. Here the quantities are never sufficient to merit separate vinification and so they become blended to give extra richness to the regular table wine.

Tony and Margaret Cox planted the vineyard 15 years ago and built a modern winery where they can make wine both for themselves and a few other small producers including Leigh Park Hotel and Little Ashley Vineyard, both near Bradford on Avon. Styles of wine include a Madeleine Angevine, a dry crisp white, a dry full-bodied Kerner, Mumfords Medium Dry white which is a blend of three grape varieties – enticingly flowery and fruity and a good party wine – and lastly, Mumfords Rosé and Mumfords Red, the latter low in tannin, made from the Triomphe grape. The wines are reckoned to be at their best between one and three years. At a Golden Jubilee luncheon attended by the Queen at the Guildhall in Bath, Mumfords Medium Dry white was selected to accompany a course of Poached Breast of Guinea Fowl, not only a great accolade for the wine but an indication that these wines drink well with white and lightly gamey meats.

There are plenty of opportunities to purchase the wines. Great Western Wines both act as their wholesale distributors and sell the wines in their retail shop in Wells Road, Bath (tel: 01225 322800). Waitrose sell the Mumfords Medium Dry white in their Bath, Bristol, Cirencester and Cheltenham branches. By far the best idea is a visit. The vineyard has become a hot venue for group tastings and it's open all the year around. Be sure to telephone first.

Oatley Vineyard

Iain and Jane Awty · Oatley Vineyard · Cannington · Bridgwater · Somerset · TA5 2NL
Tel and Fax: 01278 671340 OS Map Ref ST233398

As in other wine-producing countries, English wines are governed by the all-embracing French term *terroir*, the melting-pot effect of soil, weather, grape variety and location of vineyard. Presented with a cool climate, they tend to be fresh and herbaceous and can be marginally low in alcohol, but not so at Oatley Vineyard where the wines reach 11.5% vol. Techniques and quality of English wines have leapt ahead in recent years.

Swiss Cottage Library in 1980s London was the first source of viticultural information for Iain and Jane Awty. 'It was an impulse after a family holiday in France, we had this wheeze to buy a vineyard. The early eighties were still pre-internet and I'd been involved with computers, working for a global company. Suddenly it seemed stupid to settle for only one job in life.'

The name Oatley perpetuates the ancient title of the field in which the vineyard stands; there is tell of the Oatleghe Oak and a stone Herepath, the ancient Saxon warpath bounding the vineyard which lies between the Quantock Hills and the sea, reached by a long track leading from the A39 west of Cannington. You might be forgiven for thinking the directions to get there are something of a spoof, but the track does finally open out to reveal the familiar outlines of a vineyard to the left.

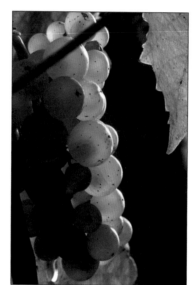

We sat under a gazebo tasting Leonora 2001. It went down a treat with its good bone-dry fruit and firm structure. Oatley grows two varieties of grapes, Kernling, said to be similar to Kerner – and Madeleine Angevine. The resultant wines are marketed as Leonora and Jane respectively. The story behind the names is that Iain fell into a badger set on Valentine's Day and broke an ankle, leaving his wife to finish the pruning alone. The wines were named after her as a thank-you.

Apart from knowledge gleaned in the Swiss Cottage Library, further Awty qualifications are a chemistry degree apiece. The rest, Iain says, is inspired guesswork. A touch over-modest because Oatley wines have won numerous awards and medals. To make the project viable and access up-to-date technology, they share equipment with other vineyards and store wine in stainless steel tanks with occasional use of oak barrels. Steve Brookshank masterminds the winemaking.

The vines dig deep into red Somerset soil and even within the five acres of vineyard, the sloping land has its own microclimate so grapes are harvested at slightly different times. Teenagers from nearby Brymore School sometimes come and help with the vintage when it coincides with the school term;

Ian Awty

indeed one batch of wine was called The Pick of Brymore, proving popular with parents and pupils. However, the harvest is only a part of the vineyard work. At the end of July when I visited, the last of the grapes were setting, the vines were being topped and de-leafed to let in light and air. Iain Awty is a serious wine maker but also a man who likes to bond with his vines, particularly he says with the Kernling because of its anarchic behaviour. Kernling makes the bigger bodied of the two varieties and is a good accompaniment to food, while Madeleine Angevine is aromatic in style, a popular grape in south-western vineyards and enjoyable as an aperitif or with a light lunch.

The vineyard yields about 500 cases of wine a year, it's marketed entirely by the Awtys and it also puts in appearances at shows such as the Royal Bath and West. Although Oatley is not a tourist vineyard, interested visitors are welcome and wines can be bought on site, but do telephone beforehand.

Simon and Melanie Shuldham

Simon and Melanie Shuldham · East Stoke House · Stoke Sub Hamdon · Somerset · TA14 6UF
Tel: 01935 823884 / 822300 Fax: 01935 824596

If Wimbledon fortnight fell a little later in June, would the spectators eat raspberries rather than strawberries? Both fruits are so deliciously redolent of summery English puddings. No matter, the loam soil of Stoke Sub Hamdon is up to the mark for production of a whole selection of fine soft fruits, namely strawberries, raspberries, tayberries, loganberries, blackberries, gooseberries and redcurrants – and in addition asparagus. No blackcurrants, though; they are too susceptible to disease for Simon Shuldham's taste and he dislikes the idea of using sprays.

Simon Shuldham grew up in a family who fruit-farmed nearby in Norton Sub Hamdon for sixty years. Ultimately the farm was sold while he was training in London to be an accountant. He returned to Stoke Sub Hamdon in 1986, launched the soft fruit business in 1995 and now grows fruit on nine acres of land. He and his wife Melanie juggle four businesses and a large family between them: an accountancy practice and the farm fall to Simon while Melanie is a practising lawyer and also runs an up-market holiday-flat business.

All the growing is done in the open without poly tunnels or greenhouses; strawberries and raspberries are planted in raised beds. Raspberry plants have quite a shallow root system and hate having their feet in water but flourish when lifted into soil with good drainage. One of the more expensive soft fruits in the shops, plants are high maintenance and suffer from a variety of soil-born diseases – the task of installing the stake posts and wiring alone adds up to £2,000 plus per acre.

Surprisingly, finding pickers has become something of a problem as student holidays begin after the peak cropping time and the influx of foreign labour, mainly central European, has fallen of late. But there's always the pleasure of 'pick-your-own'.

Choosing the latter, I set off with a punnet for the fields where a family Labrador was rolling in a patch of sunlight and greeting pickers. The Shuldhams grow two varieties of raspberry, both Scottish – Glen Ample and Tulameen. During the summer season they supply to local retail outlets including delicatessens, butchers and post offices. If you enjoy the idea of PYO, it's a good idea to ring first and check what is available. Stoke Sub Hamdon is a stone's throw from Montacute, just off the A 3088 near Yeovil. A lazy alternative is The Trading Post (*see* facing page) near South Petherton, an Aladdin's cave of local produce and/or organic produce, or Brimsmore Gardens Farm Shop on the outskirts of Yeovil. Both take a lot of Shuldham fruit.

The Trading Post

Sue Hasell and Steve Friend · The Trading Post · The Old Filling Station · Lopen Head · near South Petherton · Somerset · TA13 5JH
Tel: 01460 241666

Sue Hasell and Steve Friend are the masterminds and business partners behind the Trading Post, a derelict filling station in its previous life. The sizeable garden at the back of the premises had been used for the cultivation of blackcurrants and maize, an area they immediately designated as acreage for their new market garden. The philosophy was to create a shop with a difference, primarily for residents within a ten-mile radius and focussing on local and organic produce, much of it grown on the premises. Preparation of the land took place between September 1998 and June 1999 when the shop opened; a natural momentum swung into play and business has flourished ever since.

Sue's aim is to keep the economy within the community where possible, exemplified by the big range of local produce from bread, cheese, milk and fruit to pies and quiches, local organic meat, cob nuts and chestnuts, honey, salad and vegetables depending on season. It's a gem of a place, a bazaar of edibles to warm the heart of any cook. Steve is the gardener and possesses some of the greenest fingers in the county. Immaculately healthy rows of vegetables and salad stuff flourish under his aegis, untainted by insecticides and pesticides. Produce includes asparagus, globe and Jerusalem artichokes and pot-grown herbs, cucumber, tomatoes, brassicas, sprouts, leeks, salad leaves and potatoes. They also keep a small number of hens and ducks to glean and clean the ground. It's organic, as are the food products that are necessarily purchased from abroad for the shop: oranges, dates, jars and bottles of exotica and a selection of organic wines.

The Trading Post is not without some endearing eccentricities. Asked recently if they would like a defunct shed, they accepted with alacrity. It turned out to be a church hall, now rescued from demolition and planned as an extension of the shop. Their 1890s railway carriage is scheduled to open in 2004 as a café where customers will be able to feast on soups and dishes made from the Trading Post's own ingredients and recipes. Recently Sue and Steve restored a fifty-foot wooden greenhouse, used for rearing house and conservatory plants. Fresh-cut flowers and plants are displayed from original Covent Garden trolleys: books featuring local writers and artists, candles and pottery all have their niches. Whatever your domestic quest, The Trading Post is absolutely worth a visit. Spot the goods with yellow labels: the indication that the produce is their own.

Opening times are 8.30am-6.30pm from Monday to Saturday and 9.00am-1.00pm on Sundays.

Liz Scott

Liz Scott · Moorland Farm · Axbridge · Somerset · BS26 2BA
Tel: 01934 733341 email: moorlandfarm@btinternet.com web: www.moorlandfarm.co.uk

Liz Scott's suckler herd of Aberdeen Angus cattle are raised on the theatrical scenery of the Somerset Levels and the Mendip Hills that so typify the county's geography. One of the best vantage points from which to witness such a rapid change of set is outside her farm shop at the end of Moorland Street, off the main square in Axbridge town. On one side, stumpy willows line up along a rhine (a medieval drainage ditch) and the Levels stretch to infinity like a Dutch landscape. About turn, and the Mendips escalate to a steep backdrop for the town. Axbridge is medieval with narrow streets, houses in blues and pinks and yellows lead to the central market square with King John's Hunting Lodge on one corner and on another corner, raised on steps high above the square, stands the church of St John the Baptist with its brilliant blue plaster ceiling. The lodge has a small museum with treasures ranging from two Roman skeletons called Claudius and George, to a row of mousetraps used in the local workhouse.

Liz Scott's great-grandfather was a farmer and butcher in Axbridge and owned the land she now farms. She follows the same farming methods with her herd of 350 cattle. Sired naturally by Aberdeen Angus bulls bought from the celebrated Nightingale herd in Worcestershire, calves are born and reared on the farm, staying with their mothers for 8-10 months. The animals graze naturally with a short winter subsidy of crushed barley, hay or silage and sugar beet.

Slaughtering is done nearby and the meat is returned to the farm for butchery and hanging. Aberdeen Angus is much vaunted for its dark meat and excellent flavour, run through with white marblings of fat that adds to the tenderness in cooking. Liz Scott's house rules include treating all the animals with respect; after slaughter the beef is hung for three weeks, thus ensuring a prime product. There is no history of BSE in the herd.

Axbridge is at the beginning of the A371 that runs on through Cheddar to Wells. The farm shop is open from Monday to Saturday, 9.00am-5.30pm, or you can catch up with Moorland Farm beef at Bristol Farmers' Market outside the Exchange in Corn Street on Wednesdays and at the monthly markets in Axbridge, Cheddar, Highbridge, Clevedon, Weston-Super-Mare and Crewkerne. It's packed ready for refrigeration or freezing.

Fry's Hill

Besley's Fruits

Besley's Fruits · Merryfields · Cheddar · Somerset · BS27 3RU
Tel: 01934 741256

A black-and-white photograph taken between the two wars is pinned up in the hut where the Besleys' 'pick-your-own' strawberries are weighed. It shows fields of 'Cheddar' strawberries stretching the length and breadth of the valley from Axbridge to Draycott. Those were the days of the Strawberry Line, the nick-name for the East Somerset Railway that began running at the end of the nineteenth century, taking the fruit grown in the Cheddar Valley to the fruit markets in London. Today those fields may be down in number, but what was once a six-week season has been swapped for one that stretches from May to September, thanks to new varieties and some rotation planting. The reputation of Cheddar strawberries is still that of the best and sweetest fruit; add a dollop of cream and who in the world can resist them?

In 1974 a tragic air crash caused loss of life and serious injury to many families in the Cheddar area, and the Besleys were amongst those deeply affected. Although they had been born into a farming family, the farm was sold and two of the sons, Cliff and Phillip, went to work at the Wookey Paper Mill but took over an allotment in 1991 and began strawberry growing in their spare time. Now they've set up in partnership with Cliff's wife Mandy and are establishing an impressive acreage of fruit, to date an astonishing 100,000 plants. It's a tremendous enterprise.

Most of the fruit is grown in grow bags, Elsanta, Everest and a new variety released last year called Elan, a big juicy

fruit, luscious and deep red throughout. Strawberry growing is an around-the-year job. Not only has all the fruit to be hand picked but every plant is sown by hand. In the bleak February days, the leaves are cut right down on the plants to prevent botrytis and the plants covered with polythene to regenerate cropping.

Looking down a long line of ripe fruit I asked who, apart from human beings, helped themselves to the strawberries; there were the usual cast of slugs and greenfly but also badgers, animals deeply partial to fruit, squirrels who pick and pile them up 'just for fun' and the birds with whom the Besley family are more than happy to share a few fruits in exchange for a song.

Besley's strawberries even found their way as far as Newfoundland, ten trays being served at a feast to celebrate the arrival from Bristol of the replica ship *Matthew* in July 1997 as a tribute to John Cabot's discovery of Newfoundland 500 years earlier. Nearer home you can find them throughout the Farmers' Markets in Somerset, Wiltshire and Gloucestershire – I discovered them first in Wells Market.

At present the PYO is open on Sundays during the peak of the cropping, but it's worth telephoning to check before heading for the fields. The farm is on the right hand side of the A371 going from Cheddar to Wells, just before entering Draycott village.

Mandy, Cliff and Phillip Besley

Sedgemoor Honey

Chris Harries · Sedgemoor Honey Farm · Creech St. Michael · Somerset
Tel: 01823 442734

Chris Harries's three hundred beehives are placed from Hinkley Point to Yeovil and Forde Abbey to Cheddar, a generous cross-section of Somerset. His first taste of bee-keeping began at school in response to a compulsory activities afternoon each week, during which 'you simply couldn't get away with doing nothing'. Chris says that bees are thoroughly bad tempered when anywhere near oil seed rape; the oil seed flower produces such quantities of nectar that the bees become frenzied with overwork. Honey made from the old varieties of oil seed rape used to produce a slightly unpleasant vegetal flavour but this is no longer the case with new varieties; however, one remaining hiccup is that the honey tends to be rock-hard.

The notion of a worker bee is somehow very gratifying, a small furry insect collecting nectar to make honey, and so it's sad to discover their lives are so short. A worker bee born in the spring has a life expectancy of little more than six weeks, whereas those born in autumn live for six months. Bees will fly in a two-mile radius from the hive to search for nectar – but always in a straight line. A cautionary note – in winter bees rest and can store up their bodily fluids for up to six weeks, but come the first sunny day they leave the hive. Just ensure your washing is not in the line of fire.

Honey bees are *apis melifera*. Chris Harries reinforces his stock every year by importing from Hawaii. These arrive in little wooden boxes with three adjoining sections per box. The first section contains candy, the food for the journey; the second, the Queen Bee and ten worker bees are housed in the final section. Bees are susceptible to bacterial infection but hives are inspected regularly by the Department for the Environment, Food and Rural Affairs to forestall problems. A little thieving goes on from the hives, mainly by mice, badgers and green woodpeckers.

Bees are happiest in warm humid weather, as this is when the sugar rises in the flowers. Wet weather washes out the nectar and windy weather blows it away. Royal jelly, its constituents still defying precise analysis, is a substance produced by bees from the glands in their heads; it looks and tastes rather like yoghurt and is fed only to the Queen. Heather honey is the caviar in the bee-keeping business. Whereas other honey can be extracted in a large stainless steel centrifuge, heather honey is more jelly-like than liquid and has to be pressed. Chris suggested eating it on warm scones and with a dollop of cream on top. I did, and the explosion of flavour was sensational.

Honey must contain sixty per cent of what is stated on the jar. The varieties of Sedgemoor Honey are Clover, Borage, Heather and General Summer Flower. Some is clear and some is paddled for an hour in order to break down the sugar crystals and stop it setting hard. Stockists for these honeys include Taunton Farmers' Market, the National Trust properties Montacute House, Barrington Court and Stourhead, as well as Country Stores in Taunton, Natural Life in Crewkerne and the Wine and Cheese Shop in Wellington.

The Bay Tree Food Company

The Bay Tree Food Company · Lower Westcombe Farm · Evercreech · Shepton Mallet · Somerset · BA4 6ER
Tel: 01749 831300 web: www.thebaytree.co.uk

The name Evercreech should be in thrall to hooting owls and witchcraft. Three miles away in the hamlet of Westcombe is the home of The Bay Tree Food Company where Emma Macdonald stirs cauldrons producing home-made chutneys, relishes, marmalades, curds and salsas good enough to fulfil many a gustatory dream.

Bay Tree is in its tenth year, now fully fledged from its original kitchen-table status but staunchly remaining a cottage industry in terms of individuality and quality. Emma Macdonald's business partner Lucie Green, whose previous life was as assistant buyer in Harrods' grocery department, does the marketing. No mean feat considering Bay Tree sell to delies up and down the country from Tobermory to the Scilly Isles and have recently started to supply Waitrose.

Emma has great business-like bounce. Her training as a chef included a spell in Hong Kong and today one of her ongoing tasks is hatching up new recipes and ideas – Bay Tree likes to be ahead of the game. Two of their most popular lines are Caramelised Onions with balsamic vinegar, and Caramelised Peppers with cider vinegar. Or maybe you fancy digging into a pot of Real Ale Chutney laced with local Oakhill Best Bitter or pepping up a bowl of steaming pasta with one of their delicious sauces. Bay Tree's concentration is focused on good ingredients and the making of products without preservatives. A lot of thought has also gone into some very stylish packaging, much of it sourced from Europe

Emma Macdonald

but as Emma says, 'you don't just get quality on the outside, you get it inside too.'

Oh, and another thing. Emma Macdonald's husband runs Cedar Walk Farms – also featured in this book. The combined and imaginative food production from these two is astonishing.

Bay Tree is part of a small complex at Lower Westcombe Farm. The two other companies working from here are James's Chocolates and Westcombe Organic Cheddar cheese, also featured in this book. The little retail shop within the complex is open from Monday to Friday, 8.30am-5.30pm (tel: 01749 831300). Other Somerset outlets include: Jon Thorner Ltd, Bridge Farm Shop, Pylle, Shepton Mallet, BA4 6TA (tel: 01749 830138) and Farringtons Farm Shop, Main Street, Farrington Gurney, Bristol BS39 6UB (tel: 01761 452266).

Olive Farm Milk and Cream

Olive Farm (Babcary) Ltd · Babcary · Somerton · Somerset · TA11 7EJ
Tel: 01458 223229

Frome Farmers' Market is held in the Cheese and Grain Building on the edge of town, a genial spot on a Saturday morning. Ignore the weather and take a big shopping basket; the market is under cover and parking is nearby. The market stalls proffer a larder-full of good food and it's amongst the eggs and cheeses, meats and honey that Rosie sells Olive Farm's unpasteurised milk and thick yellow cream, also irresistible-looking crème brûlées with dark caramelised toppings, rice and bread and butter puddings and free-range quails' eggs.

For three generations the Paull family have farmed Guernsey cows on the edge of the Sparkford Vale at Babcary. The late George Paull purchased his first cows from the island, since when the family have remained loyal to the breed. The pedigree Hurdlebrook herd graze grassland in summer and are loose-housed on straw in winter, feeding on silage supplemented with a mixed ration incorporating home-grown cereals. In 1983 the Paulls started producing unpasteurised milk and cream. Just before Christmas 2003 they brought on line a wonderful Brie-style soft cheese made wholly from their Guernsey milk and sold under the Hurdlebrook banner.

Marketing by Olive Farm is enterprising and far-reaching. In addition to Frome, they sell to Jon Thorner, the butcher in Pylle, near Shepton Mallet, Lydford Stores at Lydford-on-Fosse and Supply Stores in Queen Camel. Much goes to the London Farmers' Markets, transported by Dave and his father Ken. Top chef, Antony Worrall Thompson and Dave Paull came across one another at Henley market. AWT spotted the high quality dairy produce and buys Hurdlebrook cream for his restaurant, Notting Grill, in Notting Hill Gate, London (tel: 020 7229 1500).

John Paull

The Valley Smoke House

Jonathan Newberry · The Valley Smoke House · Elton Farm · Old Wells Road · Dundry near Bristol · BS18 8NQ
Tel: 0117 935 8338 web: www.valleysmokehouse.com

If aeroplanes skim the treetops, it may well be the Valley Smoke House is in the vicinity. It's not far from Lulsgate airport. Jonathan Newberry runs the business from a converted farm building set on the hill above Dundry and a stone's throw from Arne Herbs, also mentioned in this book. As a former chef, Jonathan learned the expertise involved with smoking food when he worked at Gravetye Manor in East Grinstead, renowned almost as much for its fine ingredients as its cooking.

The fact that Jonathan Newberry has been a chef is immediately apparent. He'd just received a large delivery of salmon; the fish were filleted in a flash and bedded down in salt, prior to being marinated in oil and cold smoked. Trout were newly placed in brine and fresh mackerel queued up for the hot smoker. Jars of smoked chillies in olive oil and a heap of smoked garlic cloves stood on a shelf in the shop. Smoked cheddar, goat cheese and brie lined part of the cold store – in other words, if it can be smoked, Jonathan can do it with a consummate skill that comes from his understanding of good food. The smoked olives to be found in the Olive Shed in Bristol are his.

The specialities of the Smoke House and their treatment prior to smoking may be very varied and include marinated food such as gravadlax, but the smoking itself is direct and unchanged with time. The sawdust for the fires comes from a sawmill handling English hardwoods – Jonathan uses oak and also green oak as it burns slower. If smoked too hot, it gives a bitter flavour. The difference between hot and cold smoking is just as it sounds. Hot smoke will actually cook the food as well as curing; for cold smoking, the pipe travels a

Fresh salmon from the Orkneys

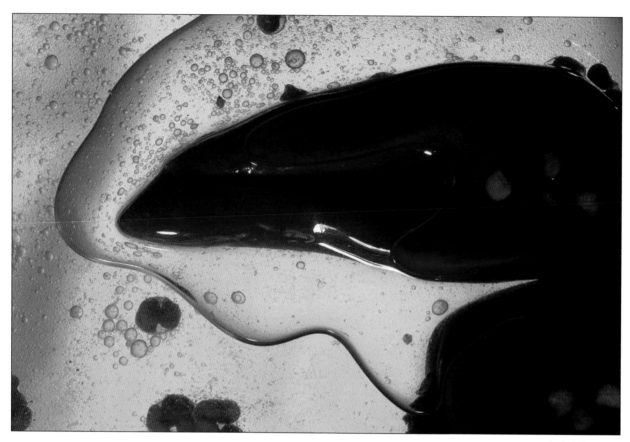

Smoked chillies

distance from the fire to smoking box and simply 'cold cures'.

The Valley Smoke House is open from Monday to Friday, but unless you are happy to take pot luck it's a good idea to ring beforehand if you want something specific. On the day I visited there were juicy-fresh scallops in from Scotland; sometimes he has diver-caught scallops and plaice from Portland. The smoked chicken is one of the best I've tasted.

The Valley Smoke House is just off the B3130.

Tony and Jane Corpe

Tony and Jane Corpe · Lower Oakley Farm · Chilthorne Domer · Yeovil · Somerset · BA22 8RQ
Tel: 01935 840567

When I telephoned Tony Corpe for the first time, the noise of low-flying aircraft drowned the conversation; the second attempt caught him in one of his hen houses. Neither set of sound effects gave the game away about his more unusual farming interest, the keeping of a herd of water buffalo. The chickens are reared as free-range table birds; the buffalo, a relatively new venture, for their meat, although initially the plan had been for them to be milked.

Tony and Jane Corpe had previously been dairy farmers for some thirty years, but seeing no future within the dairy industry, they reluctantly decided the only way forward was to sell their cows. Looking for a diversification similar to dairy cows, they purchased twenty newly weaned female water buffalo calves from Romania. Showing great panache, the Corpes put the calves through quarantine and installed them on their farm near Yeovilton. There has followed a long and gentle learning curve during which time the herd have endeared themselves to all and sundry and have settled into

Somerset life.

Romanian water buffalo are not inbred and are genetically unchanged over two thousand years; they are not to be confused with American bison or African water buffalo, larger and far more dangerous animals. Tony Corpe finds them friendlier and more intelligent than cows and is particularly impressed with the bull – christened Clinton Baldrick – because of the sense of responsibility he shows, particularly towards the calves. Should one become separated from the herd, it's the bull rather than a dizzy mother who, with a series of grunts, coaxes the calf back to the herd. The females give birth without help, and the vet's bills are negligible as the animals naturally heal quickly. The buffalo are housed during winter to avoid damaging the land.

We went to meet the herd. They responded to Tony Corpe's gentle blandishments and advanced across the field in a rhythmical sway as though performing some ritualistic dance. Unlike cows, they have sloping backs, thick skins and large feet, and to quote Stephen Morris, whose encounter was at very close quarters whilst taking the photographs, a somewhat querulous eye.

Rules for slaughter fall under the same guidelines as beef cattle; it must take place at thirty months. This is done locally and the meat is returned to the farm for a period of three weeks for hanging. Barry Barclay, a traditional butcher, prepares the joints, steaks and sausages in a time-honoured way.

The meat does not have the same marbling as beef; instead, the fat is on the outside and can be used on top of a joint for basting during cooking. The flavour is natural, quite beef-like but a little softer in texture, and being 40% lower in cholesterol is a healthy and delicious alternative to beef.

Lower Oakley Farm is just off the A37, between Ilminster and Yeovil. The buffalo meat can be purchased either in Axbridge Farmers' Market under the name of 'West Country Water Buffalo', or direct from the farm, but it is essential to telephone in advance before visiting. Cuts of meat are subject to availability but include all traditional cuts such as fillet, sirloin, rump, joints, buffalo burgers, sausages and faggots.

Westcombe Dairy

Lower Westcombe Farm · Shepton Mallet · Somerset · BA4 6ER
Tel: 01749 831300 Fax: 01749 831233 e.mail: sales@westcombedairy.co.uk web: www.westcombedairy.co.uk

Tom Calver

Westcombe Dairy looks up towards slopes of farmland grazed by a 400-strong dairy herd of Holstein cattle run by Richard Calver and his son, Tom, recently a chef in Canary Wharf. Visiting the dairy in the late morning, I was in time to see the long milk trough filled with already curded cheese, about to be sliced in rectangles. This was the result of the morning's milking, waiting for the next stage of cheese making, the cheddaring, the turning of the curd from crumbly lumps to pliable slabs. That's how fast and fresh the initial procedure is and it's one of the reasons for Westcombe's reputation as skilled makers of unpasteurised Cheddar and Westcombe Red cheese.

The company, Milton-Westcombe Ltd, was set up by Mrs P M Clothier and her husband. This is a prime area for cheese; it was at Milton Farm in Somerset that Edith Cannon won an award for the best cheese in the British Empire in the 1890s. Cheddar cheese is deeply traditional to Somerset, something Richard Calver puts down to the minerals in the soil helping to flavour the lush grass, a cause and effect that reflects on through the food chain. Although not taking an entirely organic route, he is reducing reliance on artificial nitrogen and replacing it with more clover-rich pasture. As he says, it's in his interest to be both welfare and environmentally friendly, it makes the cows happier and improves their performance.

Returning to the cheese making, once the cheese has been cheddared and pressed in stainless steel moulds, it's larded, wrapped in a muslin cloth and pressed for another night, a process of only a few days in all. Then begins the period of maturation, in the case of Westcombe Dairy up to eleven months in the cheese store where great cheddars sit in cathedral-like calm on wooden shelves in cool dark surroundings, gathering beneficial crusty moulds and fulfilling their flavour potential.

Annatto is used in the making of Westcombe Red. This is a derivative of Achiote seed and in its paste or powder form is used for food colouring, lending a light nutty flavour. This flavoursome cheese matures for four to five months and is softer than the cheddar. Westcombe Dairy is also used by Chris Duckett to make his pasteurised Caerphilly and Wedmore Caerphilly with chives.

With Neal's Yard in London, Westcombe Dairy in association with Montgomery's of Yeovil and Keens of Wincanton are part of the Slow Food Movement that began in Italy, the keynotes of which are to raise awareness about craftsmanship behind artisan food and to show consumers how to recognise and appreciate it.

The cheeses are available from the Westcombe Farm shop (tel: 01749 831800), Sagebury Cheeses, 21 Cheap Street, Frome, Somerset BA11 1BN (tel: 01373 462543); Sabins Fine Foods, 5 Hound Street, Sherborne, Dorset DT9 3AB (tel: 01935 816037); Neal's Yard, Covent Garden, London.

An Introduction to Cider

Although born in Plymouth and raised on the edge of Dartmoor, **James Crowden** has taken on the mantle of Somerset. His cider maps are an essential for those wanting to explore and imbibe one of Somerset's most celebrated products. James is a poet, food historian, prolific author, researcher and raconteur, and has been unstinting with his encouragement throughout the writing of this book. The big question is why do apples grow particularly well in Somerset? Devon, he says, was also a major apple county, but has lost 90% of its orchards since 1945. Major firms like Coates, Showerings and Taunton Cider were all Somerset-based and the county itself has a good fruit-growing climate in some of the low-lying sheltered areas. Things just evolved that way.

To include stories of all the cider producers in the county would require a separate tome, but while recounting the tale of Burrow Hill Cider and Apple Brandy, it's also essential to mention Sheppy's, Rich's, Wilkins, Hecks, Pennards, Matthew Clark and Thatchers ciders – to name but a few.

If you would like to get hold of James Crowden's ***Somerset Cider and Apple Juice, a guide to orchards and cider makers***, contact any Somerset Tourist Information Centre, or:

Somerset Visitor Centre,
Road Chef Services,
Axbridge,
Somerset, BS26 2UF
Tel: 01934 750833

The **Cider map** is available on the web at:

www.celebratingsomerset.com

Cider, The Forgotten Miracle is available from James Crowden's website:

www.james-crowden.co.uk

Somerset Cider Brandy Company

Julian Temperley · Somerset Cider Brandy Company Ltd · Burrow Hill · Kingsbury Episcopi · Martock · Somerset · TA12 5BU
Tel: 01460 240782   Fax: 01460 249220   web: www.ciderbrandy.co.uk

Burrow Hill is apple-fragrant on a mellow October day. As one turns into the premises of the Somerset Cider Brandy Company, trees in the orchards display robust fruits, mounds of gnarled red apples wait in the yard to be washed and pressed and the apple juice is flowing. Everything is on the move, including the king of West Country cider, Julian Temperley. These are pivotal weeks for the ensuing year's business and he's wired for action. Cider and Somerset have always been synonymous; however, to quote Mr Temperley, 'at last there is plenty of clear water between craft and industrial.' The good Somerset ciders made with 100% local apples are a far cry from some of the mass-produced offerings whose ingredients include, perish the thought, imported apple concentrate and glucose.

What Julian Temperley has done is to return cider to the status it deserves by giving it a purpose – in other words, reintroducing it to the dinner table. Yes, it's a great drink at the local bar with a ploughman's, but it also goes incredibly well with more complex food. One of Burrow Hill's specialities is a bone-dry single apple cider produced by utilizing the apple juice as though making champagne. The juice is fermented in bottle and ultimately goes through remuage, a riddling or hand turning to shift the sediment up to the bottleneck. The sediment is frozen and the frozen plug disgorged and replaced with cider before final corking. It takes up to two years so the yeasts have time to break down, giving the cider finely beaded bubbles and releasing a flavour that comes from the very heart of the fruit. Two rare types of cider apple are suitable for this treatment, Kingston Black and Stoke Red. The more usual rule of thumb is for cider makers to blend several different varieties of apples for an artisan cider.

Burrow Hill Pomona, a deep-gold liquid along the lines of Pineau de Charente, is another house speciality; it's a gorgeous aperitif or accompaniment to homemade apple pie or good local Cheddar; drink it like a port. Whereas ingredients for Pineau are grape juice and brandy, Pomona is a blend of apple juices and cider brandy, matured in small oak barrels and offering a good thwack of alcohol, about 20% by volume.

Perhaps the biggest adventure for Julian Temperley has been the triumph of the Somerset Cider Brandy for which he has had to fight his corner both with bureaucrats and with governments imposing punitive duties. Although it is sold in many prestigious outlets, the big coup came in the autumn of 2003 when the Scotch Malt Whisky Society took delivery of

Julian Temperley

two hogsheads of 10-year-old Somerset Cider Brandy to be sold to its members around the world. This is ultimate recognition of a top quality product.

The distilling is something Julian Temperley says he went into for romantic reasons. His curvaceous ladies, two copper stills named Fifi and Josephine, hail from Normandy where they were used to make Calvados. His cider is double distilled – as is wine in the making of Armagnac – delivering the potential for a silky-smooth apple brandy to be matured in a variety of barrels – from which it leaches its golden colour and loses a small amount of alcohol through the wood, known as the angels' share.

Somerset Cider Brandy, alias Burrow Hill Cider Farm, produce a style of drink for just about every taste ranging from pure apple juice and draught cider to Pomona, Apple Eau de Vie and the Three, Five and Ten Year Old Apple Brandy. Not forgetting of course Kingston Black Aperitif, a lighter, dryer version of Pomona, and the exuberant and elegant Single Apple bottle-fermented cider. The orchards spread around Burrow Hill and Kingsbury Episcopi, and a visit to the shop with its wooden floors and vast barrels of cider, is essential. Opening hours are Monday to Saturday from 9.00am until 5.00pm, closed on Sundays.

The Recipes

■ Starters

■ Main courses

■ Puddings

■ Drinks

Mulled cider, page 101

6 servings

Smoked eel, the very eel we have in Somerset, soused herring and salmon are particularly relished in Scandinavian countries, served either as part of a cold table or on smørrebrød, open sandwiches. In Denmark, Aeg Stand is an accompaniment to eel and other smoked or cured fish. This is a savoury egg custard, set in a bain marie and served in strips with the fish.

> 3 large free-range eggs
> 9 tbsp water
> Salt and pepper
> Butter or oil

Preheat the oven to 170°C (325°F (gas mark 3)

1 Butter or oil a small Swiss Roll tin, approximately 18 x 28 cm (7 x 11 in).

2 Whisk the eggs and water with a little seasoning, strain into a buttered dish and cover with tinfoil.

3 Set the tin in a bain marie of hot water and cook in the top of an oven for 30 minutes, or until set.

Once cooled, cut into strips to serve.

Basil Panna Cotta

A starter for 4

Creamy basil panna cotta is delicious with skinned, finely chopped tomato, chives and a scattering of young salad leaves* dressed with lemon and walnut oil.

2 tbsp water

1 heaped teaspoonful gelatine powder

300 ml (10 fl oz) single cream

15 g (½ oz) freshly grated Parmesan

25 g (a fistful) of fresh basil leaves

2 tsp lemon juice

Salt and pepper

1 Put the water into a small bowl and sprinkle the gelatine powder over the top. Leave to dissolve for 5-6 minutes.

2 Pour the cream into a pan and heat gently to just below simmering point. Remove from the heat. Stir in the dissolved gelatine and add the Parmesan cheese. Pour into a liquidiser, add the basil leaves and whizz until creamy. Add the lemon juice and seasoning to taste and divide between 4 small ramekins. Chill for 3 to 4 hours until set. To release from the ramekins, dip into hot water for a few moments.

* The Trading Post (*see* page 39) specialises in home-grown salad leaves, including nasturtium and borage flowers at the right time of the year.

Leeks with Egg and Cress Vinaigrette

4 servings

The versatile leek lends itself to stews and soups, as a vegetable and a salad. Dressed with vinaigrette and chopped egg, it's a delicious starter or accompaniment to a main course.

6 healthy looking leeks

Vinaigrette

3 tbsp extra virgin olive oil

1 tbsp white wine vinegar

1 tsp salt

Black pepper

1 tsp caster sugar

2 hard boiled eggs, finely chopped

1 box of mustard and cress

1 Trim the leeks, cut into lengths of approximately 10 cms (4 in), split horizontally. Either steam or cook in a frying pan of boiling water until tender. Run carefully under cold water, drain, gently squeeze out the excess water and arrange on a plate.

2 Whisk the oil, vinegar, salt, pepper and sugar together with a fork. Add the chopped egg. Spoon over the leeks and sprinkle with the mustard and cress.

2 lb loaf tin or a round 17 cm (7 in) cake tin

When selling a house, bake a loaf of bread – what purchaser could resist the homely smell? This recipe uses brown flour from Burcott Mill. It involves neither a bread-making machine nor the necessity to wait for a second rise in the dough. I use dough hooks with an electric whisk.

A smidgen of soft butter
450 g (1 lb) Extra Fine Burcott Mill Wholemeal Flour
1 level tsp sea salt
1 tsp Doves Farm Quick Yeast, available from all branches of Waitrose
1 tsp Malt Extract, available from Health Food shops
350 ml (12 fl ozs) warm water
1 tbsp vegetable oil

Pre-heat the oven to 220°C (425°F) gas mark 7

1 Line the bottom of the tin with baking parchment and grease the sides with the soft butter.

2 Sift the flour, sea salt and yeast in a large bowl.

3 Dissolve the malt extract with 175 mls (6 fl oz) boiling water; bring the liquid up to 350 mls (12 fl oz) with cold water and add the vegetable oil.

4 Make a well in the flour, gradually add the warm malty water, mixing in the flour as you go. Dust your hands with flour and knead the last bit by hand until the dough is pliable. Form it into roughly the shape of the baking tin and cover with lightly oiled cling film. Leave in a warm place until the dough is almost touching the cling film – it takes a couple of hours to rise.

5 Bake in the top of the oven for 40 minutes, remove from the tin and stand on a cake rack to cool. Don't try slicing until it's really cold.

Nordic Maudie's Tomato and Orange Soup

4-6 servings

Nordic Maudie, whose real name was Joan Warburton, was an East Anglian painter. It was she who introduced me to this soup. At the time of year when tomatoes are abundant and the leaves of the plants throw off that unmistakable metallic smell, it's a wonderfully refreshing starter. It's worth a trip to Arne Herbs (*see* page 7) to buy tarragon plants; once established they become healthy perennials.

 8 tomatoes, skinned but not de-seeded*

 3 sprigs fresh tarragon

 Juice of 2 oranges and the zest of one

 Juice of half a lemon

 6 spring onions, trimmed and chopped

 300 ml (10 fl oz) cold water

 Salt and pepper

 Yoghurt optional

Liquidise, chill and serve with yoghurt and a few extra tarragon leaves.

* To skin tomatoes, make a few slashes in the skin, drop into piping hot boiled water for a couple of minutes, then run under the cold tap.

a starter for 4

Colourful locally grown squashes are to be seen stacked up at greengrocers and in the Somerset markets. They yield a good orangey flesh when baked, and are delicious with butter and grated cheese, but even better with the subtle addition of smoked fish.

Choose fairly small squashes and aim to serve a half per person

2 squashes, about 500 g (1 lb 2 oz) each

450 g (1 lb) smoked cod or haddock fillet

Juice of a lemon

1 tbsp chopped flat-leafed parsley

1 tbsp Parmesan, freshly grated

2 tbsp double cream

Salt and pepper

Preheat the oven to 180°C (350°F) gas mark 4

1　Using a cleaver, cut the squashes in half, put the two halves together again: bake on a tray in the top of the oven for about 45 minutes until the flesh is soft.

2　Meanwhile cover the haddock with water and poach in a pan until lightly cooked. When sufficiently cool, drain, discard the skin and bones and put the haddock flakes into a bowl. Fold in the lemon juice, cheese, parsley and cream, add some seasoning and check the taste.

3　Scoop the seeds from the centre of the squashes and discard. Spoon the flesh into the basin and fork into the haddock mixture. Pile high into the squash shells and heat in the oven for about 20 minutes before serving.

6 servings

If you like borsht, this recipe is for you. It's made in a small loaf tin; cut it into slices to serve with soured cream and chives and strips of crisp, smoked bacon as a starter. It's also good with cold meats and salads.

450 g (1 lb) fresh or cooked beetroot

425 ml (15 fl oz) chicken, beef or vegetable stock

1 packet gelatine, sufficient for 600 ml (1 pt)

2 tbsp red wine vinegar

2 tbsp caster sugar

Zest of an orange

Salt and pepper

the sauce

140ml (5 fl oz) soured cream

Bunch of chives

1 To cook the beetroot, wash any soil from the outside and put into an ovenproof casserole with lid. Add 200 mls (7 fl oz) water and cook in the centre of an oven at 150°C (300°F) gas mark 3 for 2 to 2½ hours. Allow the beetroot to cool.

2 Peel the beetroot and either grate or cut into tiny cubes – fine grating gives the jelly a better consistency. Use the stock and make up the jelly according to instructions, add the vinegar. Stir in the caster sugar, orange zest, a little salt and pepper and finally the grated beetroot. Set the mixture in a small loaf tin and refrigerate for at least 4 hours. Serve in slices with a sauce of soured cream and chopped chives.

6-8 servings

Chicken livers cooked in this way make a smooth, rich pâté, verging on the texture of foie gras. A modest amount of wine goes into the cooking, but the remainder and more can be downed with the pâté and lots of brown toast.

> 250 g (9 oz) chicken livers from free range hens
> Bottle of Mumfords Medium Dry White Wine, available from Waitrose and other stockists*
> Butter
> Salt

Pre-heat the oven to 150°C (300°F) gas mark 2

1 Trim and discard the sinewy bits from the livers, put into an oven-proof dish and barely cover with the wine. Cover with tinfoil.

2 Set the dish in a tin of very hot water and bake in the centre of the oven for 50 minutes or until the livers are pink in the middle but set.

3 Drain and discard the liquid. Weigh the livers. Purée with a similar weight of melted butter, add a little salt and spoon into a storage bowl. When the pâté is cold, cover with a little clarified butter.**

* See the Mumfords Vineyard entry (*see* page 35) for stockists.

** To clarify butter, melt gently in a pan, let it settle, then spoon the clear butter away from the sediment at the bottom of the pan.

a starter for 4

Sourcing fresh brown shrimps in the UK isn't easy, so to find them on the doorstep in Somerset feels a triumph. Potted shrimps in butter, spiked with lemon juice and Tabasco and knifed on to buttery brown toast are one of the all-time treats. However, diligence is required in the peeling of these little dears, they are fiddly. Fresh is best, but Brendan Sellick (*see* page 31) sometimes has frozen shrimps and these too provide excellent flavour.

 450 g (1 lb) fresh brown shrimps from Brendan Sellick
 60 g (2 oz) butter
 Lemon juice
 Tabasco
 Little sea salt and black pepper

Select some thought-provoking music and peel the shrimps. Melt the butter in a saucepan; add 2 to 3 teaspoonfuls of lemon juice, 4 dashes of Tabasco and a little salt and pepper. Stir in the shrimps. Spoon into four ramekins, cover and refrigerate. To serve, stand the ramekins in hot water until the buttery mixture is melting. Make lots of brown toast.*

* To keep the shrimps for two or three days in the fridge, seal the tops of the ramekins with a little extra melted butter.

Roasted Pumpkin Purée

4 to 6 servings

It may sound a bit of a carry-on, but to savour the best flavours of pumpkin, first roast it, then purée with nutmeg and crème fraîche. This cheerful orange vegetable, grown at Charlton Orchards (*see* page 19) amongst other places in Somerset, is particularly good with gamey roast meats such as pheasant and partridge, and as an accompaniment to baked or grilled fish. A cleaver is the most effective implement with which to chop it, good value in Chinese supermarkets!

>2 kilos (4 lbs 8 oz) of pumpkin (about half a medium-sized pumpkin)
>Vegetable oil
>2 tbsp crème fraîche
>1 tbsp freshly grated Parmesan cheese
>Freshly grated nutmeg
>2 tsp lemon juice
>Salt and pepper

Preheat oven to 190°C (375°F) gas mark 5

1 Chop the pumpkin into pieces approx. 10 cm x 10 cm (4 in x 4 in), scoop away the seeds and coarse fibres. Paint with vegetable oil and roast flesh-side-up on a baking tray for 45-55 minutes until soft and just beginning to brown.

2 Slice the flesh from the skin, put into a food processor or mash with the crème fraîche, Parmesan cheese, a grating of fresh nutmeg and salt and pepper. Taste to check seasoning.

Alexis Gauthier, chef of Rousillion Restaurant (16 Barnabas Street, London SW1 W8PE, tel: 020 7730 5550) suggests pan-frying the spears in a little smoking hot olive oil for 20-30 seconds, giving them a good shake and then adding a splash of water and covering the pan with a lid. The asparagus steams while the water condenses on the lid and recycles. After three minutes or so the asparagus is cooked and the water absorbed. Cooking is perfect when the asparagus stems yield a little to the fingertips.

If the idea of butter, sea salt, pepper and shavings of fresh parmesan seems more atttractive, in the absence of an asparagus steamer I use a large frying pan of lightly salted water and cook the asparagus with the tips away from the heat source. They take about ten minutes.

Cooked asparagus spears are always a bonus to salads: raw asparagus chopped into salad is an exciting and delicious surprise, the flavour more akin to raw peas.

Cheese Pudding

6 servings

With the distinct advantage that it's less temperamental than soufflé, this is an easy-going lunchtime or supper dish. Use the best mature cheddar. I cook it in a Pyrex dish, approximately 20 cm (8 in) in diameter.

1 tsp English mustard powder

600ml (1 pint) whole milk

1 tsp cayenne pepper

4 large eggs, whites and yolks separated

175g (6 oz) fresh white bread crumbs (good bread, not flabby sliced white)

200g (7 oz) mature cheddar cheese, grated

Salt and pepper

Butter for greasing baking dish

Pre-heat the oven to 190°C (375°F) gas mark 5

1 Spoon the mustard in a basin, stir in 1 tablespoonful of the milk plus the cayenne pepper and egg yolks.

2 Bring the milk up to simmering point in a saucepan, stir in the breadcrumbs and leave to cool for 5 minutes.

3 Mix together the milk and egg yolk mixture, followed by the grated cheese and a little salt and pepper. Butter the baking dish.

4 Whisk the egg whites, fold into the cheese mixture and pour into the baking dish. Cook in the oven for 35 to 40 minutes until golden. Serve warm.

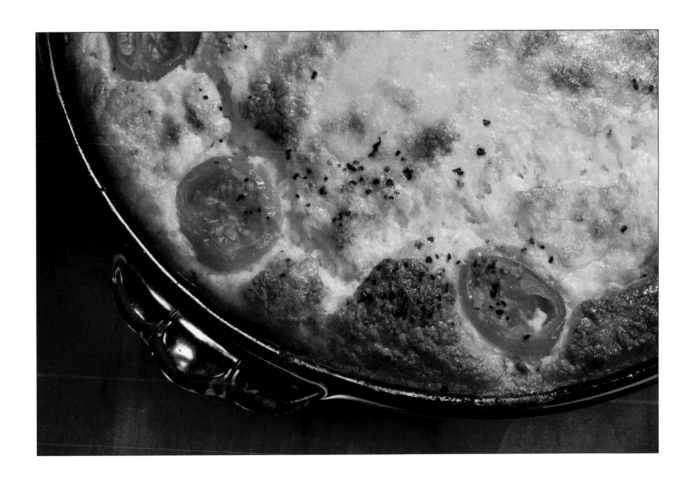

Pork Tenderloin with Cider, Mustard and Fried Parsley

for 4

Apple and pork are one of nature's natural flavour marriages. Chopped fried parsley has a distinctive crispy texture and taste, approaching that of Chinese seaweed – itself supposedly a very finely shredded cabbage.

    600g (1 lb 5 oz) pork tenderloin
    2 tbsp chopped parsley
    1 tbsp sunflower oil
    25g butter
    200mls (7 fl oz) dry farmhouse cider
    1 tsp wholegrain mustard
    3 tbsp crème fraîche

1 Trim any sinew from the pork, cut into rounds about 1 cm (1/4 in) in thickness.

2 Heat the sunflower oil in a small pan and fry the parsley until crisp and deep green but not burnt.

3 Melt the butter in a large pan. Fry the pork gently for 3 to 4 minutes each side and lift into a warm dish.

4 Add the cider and mustard to the pan, blending the mustard in with a wooden spoon. Spoon in the crème fraîche, bring the mixture to bubbling point whilst stirring, reduce for a couple of minutes and lift the pork back into the sauce. Cook for a further minute. Add salt.

Gammon and Steak Loaf

6-8 servings

Thanks to the excellence of the pork and beef produced in Somerset, it feels fully justifiable to include this recipe from the late Mrs Mary Taylor of Elsdon, Northumberland. It is the simplest recipe imaginable; the only requisites are fine ingredients and hungry people. I like it served with either a grainy mustard sauce or mild, fruity chutney such as apricot or peach*.

   450g (1lb) rump steak
   450g (1lb) uncooked bacon, green or cured
   225g (8ozs) stale white breadcrumbs
   Salt, pepper and ground nutmeg or mace
   2 large free range eggs, lightly beaten
   Small knob of butter to grease the tin

Pre-heat the oven to 150C (300F) gas mark 2

1 Mince the two meats. Mix with the breadcrumbs, season and add the beaten egg, stirring thoroughly.

2 Butter a basin or loaf tin. Pack in the meat mixture, cover with tinfoil or a lid and stand in a bain marie. Cook in the centre of the oven for 3 hours. It's preferable to keep in the fridge overnight before cutting into slices.

* To make a mustard sauce, mix two tablespoonfuls of mayonnaise with a teaspoonful of grainy mustard.

Gremolata

4 servings

A favourite green sauce, ideal with buffalo meat

The cooking of water buffalo meat follows the same principles as cooking beef, be it the tender steaks or a big family roast. Use identical timings as you would with beef. Buffalo meat is very lean and without the fatty marbling of beef, so it may be a good idea to put a little fat on top prior to roasting, or to cover the top of the meat half way through cooking to prevent it drying out. I peeled and finely diced an onion, turned it in a tablespoonful of sunflower oil, seasoned it and spread the onion over the meat. This added flavour to the meat and the subsequent gravy.

I am a devotee of Italian Gremolata sauce served with roast or grilled meat, although my version is slightly bastardised by the addition of olive oil. It worked wonderfully well with buffalo meat.

> A large bunch of flat leaf parsley
> 2 garlic cloves
> Zest of a whole lemon and the juice of half a lemon
> 4 tbsp olive oil
> 1 level tsp sea salt

1 Chop the parsley, peeled garlic cloves and sea salt together with the lemon zest.

2 Put into a basin, stir in the olive oil and 2 tsps lemon juice, plus a little more salt if necessary. Ladle generous spoonfuls alongside the meat.

Hot Redcurrant and Walnut Vinaigrette

4 servings

This is a delicious dressing with which to deglaze the roasting pan after cooking lamb or game, to make a dark, rich gravy. It also works well with grilled trout.

2 tbsp walnut oil

50g (2 oz) chopped walnuts

125g (4 1/2 oz) red currants, destemmed

2 tbsp balsamic vinegar

2 tbsp dark muscovado sugar

4 tbsp water

Heat the walnut oil in a frying pan, add the walnuts and cook over a low heat for two minutes. Toss in the red currants and cook for a further minute. Stir in the remaining ingredients and simmer for 2 or 3 minutes to reduce it slightly. If using as a gravy, add the vinaigrette to the meat pan and incorporate the juices.

for 6

In order to be classified as mutton, the sheep will have walked a long way so gentle and lengthy cooking is essential. The rewards are a flavoursome winter dish dressed in a rich and silky cider sauce, laced with capers and parsley. Caper and parsley sauce is a traditional sidekick to mutton. I also like it with mature legs of lamb. Serve with rosemary potatoes (*see* page 90).

Cooking the mutton

A leg of mutton
Litre bottle medium-dry cider
1 bay leaf
1 parsnip, 1 carrot, 1 onion, 1 leek

Sauce

Stock from the cooked mutton, made up to 425 ml (15 fl oz) with the remaining cider
2 egg yolks
140 ml (5 fl ozs) double cream
2 tbsp capers, chopped
2 tbsp chopped parsley
Salt and pepper

Preheat the oven to 230°C (450°F) gas mark 8

1 To cook the mutton, trim away the excess fat from the meat. Peel and chop the vegetables and scatter around the baking tin. Add the mutton and pour in 200 mls (7 fl oz) of cider.

2 Cook on the top shelf of the oven for 20 minutes. Cover the tray with tinfoil, sealing the edges as much as possible. Turn the oven down to 150°C (300°F) gas mark 2, put the mutton in the bottom of the oven and cook for 4 hours.

3 To make the sauce, remove the mutton to a warm plate. Strain the juices into a measuring jug and make up to 425 mls (15 fl oz) with some of the remaining cider. Allow the stock to settle and spoon the fat from the top. Bring the stock to simmering point in a saucepan, boil for 5 minutes, skim and remove from the heat.

4 Whisk together the egg yolks and cream, add slowly to the stock and keep stirring. Put the pan on a low heat and continue stirring until the sauce thickens, fold in the chopped capers and parsley. Remove from the heat, taste and add the necessary salt and pepper. Carve the meat in thick slices, serve with the caper sauce – and the remainder of the cider as an accompaniment.

Somerset Chicken in Cider

for 4

The assembling of this dish happens in a trice. Moreover, it is very good and needs little accompaniment other than perhaps mashed potatoes with spring onions, butter and milk, in the style of the Irish Champ potatoes.

4 free-range chicken legs or thighs, or a large bird chopped into eight pieces

4 cloves of garlic

2 tbsp chopped parsley

1 tbsp olive oil

150 ml (5 fl oz) Somerset dry cider

1 jar Bay Tree Caramelised Peppers*

Juice of a lemon

Salt and pepper

Preheat the oven to 180°C (350°F) gas mark 4

1 Skin and joint the chicken legs.

2 Peel and finely chop the garlic. Mix with a tablespoonful of chopped parsley and some salt and pepper, spread over the bottom of an oven-proof casserole.

3 Arrange the chicken pieces over the top and add the cider. Scatter a generous table-spoonful of caramelised peppers over the chicken, sprinkle with the remaining parsley and add the lemon juice. Season with a little black pepper and some sea salt. Cover and cook for 70 minutes.

* For availability of Caramelised Peppers, *see* the entry for The Bay Tree Food Company on page 44.

for 4

The fragrance of the rosemary, the explosion of potato par-roasted with olive oil and seasoned with sea salt ensures this dish complements almost anything from roast meats to baked eggs.

600 g (1 lb 5 oz) small or medium potatoes
Olive oil
Sprig of rosemary, roughly chopped
Sea salt

Preheat the oven to 220°C (425°F) gas mark 7

1 Scrub the potatoes with their skins on, halve if on the large size. Steam or boil for about 20 minutes.

2 Oil the bottom of a baking dish and add the potatoes. Bash gently with the back of a wooden spoon or pestle, just to explode the skins. Drizzle a little olive oil over the potatoes, sprinkle with sea salt and the rosemary. Bake for about 45 minutes until the edges of the potato are crisp.

for 4-6

The invention of Eton Mess must have been the consequence of a schoolboy lark with a bowl of meringues, strawberries and cream. However, apart from plucking warm fruit from the plant and eating it on the spot, I think it's the most sybaritic way to enjoy the fruit.

500g (1lb 2oz) strawberries
6 tsp caster sugar
300ml (10floz) whipping cream
2 tbsp Somerset Apple Brandy
8 meringues

1 Put 200g (7oz) of the strawberries into a liquidizer with 2 teaspoonfuls of sugar and whizz to make a purée.

2 Whip the cream until it flops in folds, add 2 teaspoonfuls of sugar and the brandy. Whip a little more until the brandy incorporates into the cream.

3 An hour before pudding time, cut up the remaining strawberries and sprinkle with 2 teaspoonfuls of sugar.

4 Just before serving, crumble 8 meringues into the cream, fold in the strawberries and trickle a little of the purée over the top. Use the remainder to pour on each portion.

Apple and Blackberry Pie

6 servings

An array of dahlias, early winter leeks and windfall apples in the garden are the reminder to pick hedgerow blackberries and start baking. Blackberry and apple pie is an all-time great British pudding, the fruit cooked between crusty layers of homemade pastry, and served with real custard or clotted cream. I like to make the pie on an enamel or glass plate rather than using a deep dish.

pastry
60g (2 ozs) wholemeal flour
175g (6 ozs) plain white flour
60g (2 ozs) butter with extra for buttering the base
60g (2 ozs) lard
pinch of salt
ice cold water
a little milk and sugar to glaze the top

filling
500 g (1 lb 2 ozs) cooking apples
120 g (4 ozs) blackberries
85 g (3 ozs) caster sugar

Pre-heat the oven to 200°C (400°F) gas mark 6

1 Peel, core and finely slice the apples and put into a pan with 3 tbsp water and the caster sugar. Bring to simmering point and cook with a lid on the pan over a low heat for 4 minutes, add the blackberries and continue cooking until the apple is soft but not pulpy. Let the fruit cool.

2 Sift the flours with the salt into a mixing bowl. Rub in the butter and lard with your fingertips and add 1 - 2 tablespoonfuls of iced water, mixing with a knife blade or fingers until the pastry is cohesive. Cover the pastry with cling film and rest in the fridge for half an hour – it stops it shrinking from the edge of the plate.

3 Butter the baking plate. Roll out half the pastry to make the base, spoon the fruit into the centre leaving a 2 cm (3/4 in) margin round the edge, paint this with milk. Roll the pastry lid and cover the tart, pressing the two outside edges together and knifing off the ragged bits. Make a scalloped edge with fingertips or the end of a knife handle, and use any pastry trimmings to decorate the top. Brush some more milk over the top of the tart, sprinkle with caster sugar and make a few cuts or fork holes to let the steam escape during cooking. Bake for 35-40 minutes. Serve warm or cold.

6 servings

Cool from the fridge and served with the dark wine sauce and thick cream, spiced pears make a great pudding after a rich main course.

6 firm Conference pears

150 ml (5 fl oz) water

100 g (3 1/2 oz) soft brown sugar

2 cinnamon sticks

6 cardamom pods

third of a bottle of red wine

2 tsp corn flour

1 Peel the pears whole. Bring the water, sugar, cinnamon and crushed cardamom to simmering point and stir until the sugar dissolves, add the wine. Turn down the heat and add the pears. Simmer gently for approximately 30 minutes, turning from time to time.

2 Spoon the pears into a bowl. Strain the juices into a small saucepan. Mix the corn flour with a tablespoonful of water, stir into the juice and continue stirring until the syrup thickens and clears. Pour over the pears. Serve cold with dollops of cream.

Apple and Hazelnut Pastries

makes a dozen

The Cox's Orange Pippin is Britain's favourite apple, raised from a pip in a Ribston Pippin by Richard Cox in Slough in 1825. Unlike most eating apples, it cooks well and is particularly good for tarts and pastries. The apple in this recipe is baked on flaky pastry, a light, buttery triumph if homemade.

pastry

200 g (7 oz) plain flour

25 g (1 oz) lard

125 g (4 ½ oz) butter at room temperature

pinch of salt

4-5 tbsp cold water

fruit

3 Cox's apples

Caster sugar

Ground cinnamon

1 tbsp blanched hazelnuts, roughly chopped

25g (1 oz) butter, melted

Icing sugar for dusting the biscuits

Preheat the oven to 220°C (425°F) gas mark 7

1 To make flaky pastry, sift the flour into a large bowl. Rub 25g (1 oz) lard and 25g butter into the flour with your fingertips. Add the cold water, a tablespoonful at a time, and mix with a knife blade until the dough is cohesive. Using a floured board, roll the dough into a rectangle approximately 30cm x 15cm (12 x 6in). Spread with 50g (2 ozs) butter, leaving a narrow unbuttered border around the edges. Fold the pastry into three, butter side inwards. Repeat the rolling process again and use the remaining butter. Chill the pastry in cling film for 30 minutes.

2 Roll out the pastry and make 12 circles with a pastry cutter. Quarter the apples, remove the core and cut the fruit into thin slices. Arrange 3 pieces on each pastry. Sprinkle with a third of a teaspoonful of caster sugar, a good pinch of cinnamon and a few hazel nuts. Spoon a little melted butter on each and cook on a baking tray for 30 minutes in the top of the oven.

Serve warm with a dusting of icing sugar. These are delicious for tea, or served as a pudding with a spoonful of cream.

Plum, Stem Ginger and Yoghurt Ice Cream

6 servings

Chopped stem ginger gives a delicious kick to the plums. Although it's easier to make this in an ice-cream maker, as an alternative the mixture can be poured into a suitable bowl, frozen for an hour, whisked and frozen again.

> 500 g (1 lb 2 oz) sweetened stewed plums (Victoria or Marjorie's seedlings are best)*
> 3 knobs of stem ginger
> 500 g (18 fl oz) whole milk live yoghurt
> 2 tsp caster sugar
> 1 tbsp stem ginger syrup

1 Remove the stones from the cooked plums and finely chop the pieces of ginger.

2 Blend the plums, yoghurt, sugar and ginger syrup. Fold in the ginger and paddle the mixture in an ice-cream maker for 20 minutes. Freeze. Remove from freezer for half an hour before serving.

A little Sloe Gin poured over the top is highly recommended.

* Cooking plums

To cook the plums, put 200 g (7 oz) of granulated sugar with sufficient water just to cover the bottom of the saucepan. Stew gently with lid on pan until the fruit is cooked.

serves 6

Alluringly rich ice cream with which to finish a meal. In the absence of an ice cream maker, freezing and blending works well.

300 ml (10 fl oz) single cream
4 free range egg yolks
3 tbsp runny honey
300 ml (10 fl oz) double cream
Juice of half a lemon
3 tbsp Somerset Apple Brandy

1 Heat the single cream in a pan until simmering point, then remove from the heat. Whisk the egg yolks and honey in a china basin, place the basin over a pan of gently boiling water. Add the single cream, stirring as you go until the mixture thickens and becomes a custard that will coat the back of a wooden spoon. Remove from the heat and allow it to cool. Stir occasionally.

2 Whip the double cream until it makes thick folds, stir in the lemon juice and whisk gently to incorporate the two. When the custard is cool, mix everything together and either put into an ice cream maker or into a bowl suitable for the freezer.

3 Freeze for 3 hours and blend to break down the ice crystals. Scoop into a container with a lid and re-freeze until required.

Raspberry Sauce

for 4

Simple to make, sensational to taste. It's ideal on ice cream, chocolate puddings, fruit salads, or frozen just to the point where it reaches water ice status.

250 g (9 oz) fresh raspberries

1 tbsp icing sugar

Put the raspberries in a liquidiser with the icing sugar, whiz and rub through a sieve.

makes about a dozen glasses

For my money, mulled cider is cleaner and a much more attractive winter warmer than mulled wine.

2 litres (3½ pts) strong dry cider

1 litre (1¾ pts) apple juice

4 tbsp light brown sugar

2 cinnamon sticks

1 tsp cloves

6 slices of fresh ginger root

1 large fresh orange, sliced

1 eating apple, sliced

3-4 tbsp Somerset Apple Brandy

With the exception of the brandy, put everything into a large, heavy-bottomed pan and let the ingredients steep in the cider until the time comes to heat it up. Stir occasionally to prevent the sugar from catching the bottom of the pan and bring slowly to just below simmering point, but don't let it boil. That burns off the alcohol! Add the brandy and serve.

Sloe Gin

Pick a good walking day in October, by which time sloes are ready for picking. The more sloes you pick, the bigger the bill for gin or vodka, but it makes a great Christmas present and is stupendously good poured over plum ice-cream or spooned into a bowl of fresh strawberries or raspberries with a sprinkling of sugar. Each sloe needs to be pricked with a needle to allow the juices to flow, but if it's not a convenient task on the day of harvest, bung them in the freezer and do it at your leisure.

450 g (1 lb) sloes
75 cl bottle of gin or vodka
200 g (7 oz) granulated sugar

Remove any stalks and prick the sloes. Put them into a large kilner jar with a lid – I use an old-fashioned sweet jar – add the sugar and give it a shake. Pour in the gin and store in a cool, dark place. Shake from time to time. The sloe gin will be ready for drinking within three months. Filter the clear liquid into a bottle.

Farmers' Markets

What is a Farmers' Market?

This is the definition issued by the National
Association of Farmers' Markets:

> A Farmers' Market is one in which farmers, growers
> or producers from a defined local area are present
> in person to sell their own produce, direct to the
> public. All products sold should have been grown,
> reared, caught, brewed, pickled, baked, smoked or
> processed by the stallholder.

In other words, the pleasure of a Somerset Farmers'
Market is to buy fresh, good-quality food direct from
the person who has produced it. The food is grown or
produced within a 50-mile radius of the market so
your support goes to the local community.

For further information call: 01458 830801, or visit:
www.somersetfarmersmarkets.co.uk

Roger White

Farmers' Market Manager for Somerset

Roger was a pig farmer for thirty years, things got
more difficult and prices dropped. He tried co-opera-
tives, joining pressure groups and lobbying London
and Brussels, but finally concluded there could be
direct benefit from direct marketing. After a run of six
months as a stallholder and with farming experience
behind him, the opportunity arose for a position as
Farmers' Market Manager.

Roger White

Schedules for the Farmers' Markets

Please check times before making a special journey to the market. Locations and days can change, particularly around the time of festivals and bank holidays.

For further general information, ring Roger White on 01458 830801, or consult: www.somersetfarmersmarkets.co.uk

Axbridge

The Market Place

First Saturday of each month

9.00am until 1.00pm

Bath

Green Park Station

First and third Saturday of the month

9.00am until 2.00pm

Bridgwater

Town Centre

Second Friday of each month

9.00am until 2.00pm

Bristol

Corn Street

Every Wednesday

9.00am until 2.00pm

Chard

The Guildhall

Fourth Friday of each month

9.00am until 2.00pm

Cheddar

Church House or Cliff St. Car Park

Third Saturday of each month

9.00am until 1.00pm

Crewkerne

Falkland Square,

Town Centre

Third Saturday of each month

9.00am until 1.00pm

Frome

Cheese and Grain Building

Second Saturday of each month

9.00am until 1.00pm

Glastonbury

St John's Car Park

Fourth Saturday of each month

9.00am until 1.00pm

Highbridge

Community Hall,

Market Street

First Friday of each month

9.00am until 1.00pm

Midsomer Norton

New to the Farmers' Market scheme.

No regular dates available at time of publication

Minehead

URC Church Hall

Bancks Street

First and third Friday of each month

9.00am until 2.00pm

Taunton

High Street

Every Thursday

9.00am until 3.00pm

Wells

The Market Place

A Farmers' Market is part of

the weekly street market.

Every Wednesday

9.00am until 2.30pm

Wincanton

The Memorial Hall

First Friday of each month

9.00am until 1.00pm

Useful Addresses and Telephone Numbers

Bar Chocolat
James Chocolates
19 The Mall,
Clifton,
Bristol, BS8 4JG
Tel: 0117 974 7000
   and
8 Argyll Street,
Bath, BA2 4BS
Tel: 01225 446060

Bath Fine Cheese Company
Somerset cheeses
29 & 31 Walcot Street,
Bath, BA1 5NB
Tel: 01225 483407

Brockley Farm Shop
Local meat, vegetables, cheese, draught cider
Main Road,
Brockley, BS48 3AT
Tel: 01275 462753

Chandos Delicatessens
Somerset cheeses
12 George Street, Bath, BA1 2EA
Tel: 01225 314418
   and
6 Princess Victoria Street,
Clifton, Bristol, BS8 3BP
Tel: 0117 974 3275

The Cheese and Wine Shop
Sedgemoor Honey
11 South Street,
Wellingon,
Somerset, TA21 8NR
Tel: 01823 662899

The County Stores
Eggs from Andrew Gabriel
52 North Street,
Taunton, TA1 1ND
Tel: 01823 272235

Gerald David, Butcher
Pork from Steve Crossman, Asparagus grower
Main Shop: 3 Park Street,
Minehead,
Somerset, TA24 5NQ
Mail order Freephone: 0800 731 8231

Farmers' Markets
Roger White 01458 830801
(Bath) James Pavitt 01225 787914

Kitchens (Catering Utensils) Ltd
An Aladdin's Cave for cooks
167 Whiteladies Road,
Bristol, BS8 2SQ
Tel: 0117 923 9614
   and

4 & 5 Quiet Street,
Bath, BA1 2JS
Tel: 01225 481676

The Larder
Exmoor Jersey Blue
Fore Street,
Wellington, TA21 8AG
Tel: 01823 667992

Paxton and Whitfield
Somerset cheeses
1 John Street,
Bath, BA11 2JL
Tel: 01225 466640

Pumpkin Delicatessen, Polly Relf
Lighthouse Ice cream, Rookery Farm Clotted Cream,
Capricorn Goat Cheese, Westcombe Dairy cheeses
2 King Alfred Mews,
Church Street, Wedmore,
BS28 4AB
Tel: 01934 713289

Riverside Butchers
Eggs from Andrew Gabriel
8 Riverside Place,
2 St James's Street,
Taunton, TA1 1JH
Tel: 01823 289097

Sabins Fine Foods
Westcombe Dairy Cheese
5 Hound Street,
Sherborne,
Dorset, DT9 3AB
Tel: 01935 816037

Sagebury Cheeses
Westcombe Dairy Cheese
21 Cheap Street,
Frome,
Somerset, BA11 1BN
Tel: 01373 462543

Sara's Dairy
Exmoor Jersey Blue Cheese
2 The Cornhill,
Bridgwater, TA6 3BU
Tel: 01278 456999

Somerset Farm Direct
The Woods' family farm rears and sells lamb, pork, beef, duck,
chicken and mutton. **Mail order only**
Bittescombe Manor,
Wiveliscombe, TA4 2DA
Tel: 01398 371387
www.somersetfarmdirect.co.uk

Somerset Food Links
Tel: 01458 830801
www.somerset.foodlinks.org.uk

Somerset Tourist Board
Tel: 01823 355255
www.celebratingsomerset.com

Somerset Visitors' Centre
Road Chef Services,
Axbridge, BS26 2UF
Tel: 01934 750833

South Somerset District Council (Tourism)
Tel: 01935 462641

Jon Thorner, Butcher
Hurdlebrook Unpasteurised Cream
Bridge Farm Shop,
Pylle, Near Shepton Mallet, BA4 6TA
Tel: 01749 830138

Waitrose Supermarkets
Throughout the country

Wallaces' Farm Shop
Eggs from Andrew Gabriel
Hill Farm,
Cullompton,
Devon, EX15 3UZ
Tel: 01823 680307

Winsham Sub Post Office and General Stores
A village shop run as a co-operative by local people.
Aims to sell local produce
Church Street
Winsham,
Near Chard
Tel: 01460 30225

Acknowledgements

Stephen Morris, whose wit and observations via his camera are apparent throughout the book, and whose company and support has been a joy. Trevor Hockey, owner of the Clifton Bookshop, key player in helping me find a publisher, and for his ongoing interest in the project. Kitchens (Catering Utensils) Bristol,* which lent a fine selection of dishes and plates for the food shots. Nicholas McClean, my ever-patient husband, for playing the role of taster-in-chief. Veronica Rodwell, earliest and most literate school friend, who read, advised, and struck out the stray apostrophes. John Sansom of Redcliffe Press who by his *laissez-faire* approach and total support, allowed the book to develop its character, unhindered.

* See the Directory for addresses

Andrea Leeman, Bristol, March 2004

The photographs in this book exist because so many people responded to our requests for access with unaffected kindness and enthusiasm. We thank them all. The animals, though less co-operative, were never spiteful.

Stephen Morris

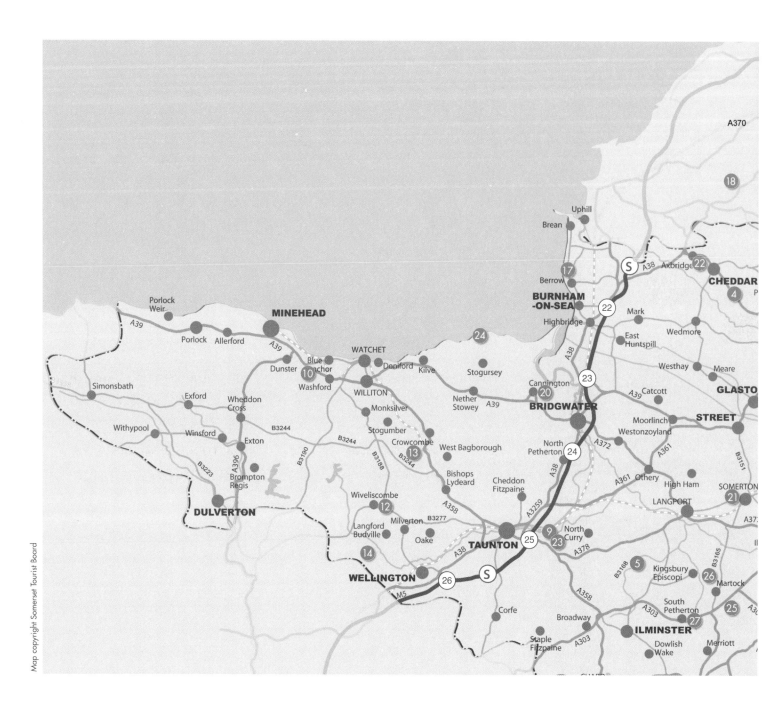

Map copyright Somerset Tourist Board

Map of the Sites

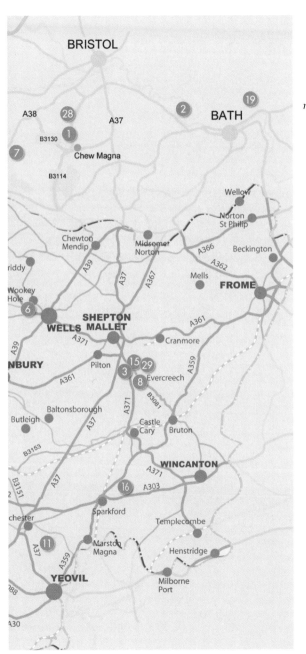